SUPER WOMEN

Six Scientists Who Changed the World

Laurie Lawlor

HOLIDAY HOUSE ★ NEW YORK

Spectacular first view of the Earth from the *Freedom 7* capsule on May 5, 1961. Astronaut Alan B. Shepard Jr.'s history-making suborbital flight was a success thanks to mathematician Katherine Coleman Johnson and a team of "computers."

For Vivian Elise Beaudoin

Copyright © 2017 by Laurie Lawlor
All Rights Reserved
HOLIDAY HOUSE is registered in the U.S. Patent and Trademark Office.
Printed and Bound in March 2017 at Worzalla, Stevens Point, WI, USA.
www.holidayhouse.com
First Edition
1 3 5 7 9 10 8 6 4 2
Library of Congress Cataloging-in-Publication Data

Names: Lawlor, Laurie.
Title: Super women : six scientists who changed the world / by Laurie Lawlor.
Description: First edition. | York, PA : Holiday House, [2017] | Audience:
Age 8–12. | Audience: Grade 4 to 6.
Identifiers: LCCN 2016027036 | ISBN 9780823436750 (hardcover)
Subjects: LCSH: Women scientists—Biography—Juvenile literature. | Scientists—Biography—Juvenile literature.
Classification: LCC Q141.L4235 2017 | DDC 509.2/52—dc23 LC record available at https://lccn.loc.gov/2016027036

TABLE OF CONTENTS ☆ ☆ ☆

INTRODUCTION   v

1 EUGENIE CLARK   1

2 GERTRUDE ELION   8

3 KATHERINE COLEMAN JOHNSON   16

4 MARIE THARP   23

5 FLORENCE HAWLEY ELLIS   31

6 ELEANOR MARGARET BURBIDGE   41

   ACKNOWLEDGMENTS   50

   GLOSSARY   51

   SOURCES   53

   SOURCE NOTES   55

   PICTURE CREDITS   57

   INDEX   58

Genie Clark, pictured here in the late 1950s, often commented on the helpful knowledge of local fishermen when she dove to explore fish populations around the world.

INTRODUCTION

IMAGINE being a highly trained astronomer who's forbidden to look through a state-of-the-art telescope, or an accomplished underwater cartographer who's not allowed to sail on research ships. Imagine graduating with honors in chemistry but being told you're "too distracting" to work in the research laboratory. All because you happen to be a woman.

Pioneering scientists Eleanor Margaret Burbidge, Marie Tharp, and Gertrude Elion experienced such thunderbolts of discrimination more than half a century ago. Florence Hawley Ellis, who forged her career as an archaeologist in the inhospitable Southwest United States in the 1930s, was told point-blank that men would refuse to work for a female boss on her first organized dig. Mathematician Katherine Coleman Johnson and marine biologist Eugenie Clark faced double prejudice as women of color. Johnson, an African American, was initially relegated to a segregated office area when she began work as a "human computer" for what later became the National Aeronautics and Space Administration (NASA). Japanese American Clark faced interrogation by the FBI as a possible alien terrorist following World War II and was forced to forfeit a research expedition to the Philippines.

These six super women shared a passion for discovery and a love of science in spite of daunting obstacles. Again and again they were forced to leap over academic, societal, and professional barriers, and they did so with remarkable courage, energy, and endurance. What made these six scientists super women was not just their rigorous minds, quest for knowledge, and ability to learn from mistakes, it was also the way they tirelessly mentored and inspired confidence in the next generations of young women scientists. Their advice is perhaps best summed up by Nobel Prize Laureate Trudy Elion, who once said, "Do not let anyone discourage you."

While enormous strides continue to be made in the twenty-first century, women and individuals of color sometimes still encounter subtle discouragement and prejudice in the sciences. Much remains to be accomplished to ensure that collaborative scientific research includes the broadest spectrum of perspectives. "The future of our country increasingly depends on science and technology," writes Meg Urry, the Israel Munson Professor of Physics and Astronomy at Yale University and the Director of the Yale Center for Astronomy and Astrophysics. "We need all the best brains, regardless of gender."

Genie Clark, pictured inside the jaws of a great white, proved sharks were far more intelligent than anyone had realized.

CHAPTER ONE

Eugenie CLARK

The 13-ton whale shark swam straight for Eugenie "Genie" Clark and the three other scuba divers. Its open mouth was so enormous it could easily have swallowed all four of them at once. Suddenly, the city bus–size creature veered away. As it did it peered at Genie for a moment through one great dark eye rimmed with white. The shark's benign glance inspired the 59-year-old scientist to do something few would have dared.

She decided to take the ride of her life.

She flippered closer. Ducking under the massive pectoral fin that projected like an aircraft wing, Genie trailed her fingers along the rough side of the whale shark. White dots as big as her hand adorned its thick, elephant-like hide. Quickly, she propelled herself upward to the shark's back and grabbed the soft trailing edge of its dorsal fin.

The whale shark plunged with enormous, slow beats of its tail. Like a jockey, Genie pulled up her knees and sat astride the shark's emery-board back. The biggest

known species of fish in the world picked up speed. Faster, faster.

Water pressed against Genie's face. If she turned her head to try to spot her distant companions or the dive boat, she feared that her diving mask would rip away. Her hands began to cramp. Scraped skin on her inner legs stung. She adjusted position, lowered herself onto her belly, and slid past the rear dorsal fin to the immense tail. She hung on as she was whiplashed from side to side before being catapulted free.

Unharmed, she floated to the surface. Her scuba tank had come loose. She'd lost a flipper, and her mask dangled from her neck. No matter. Eagerly, Genie took one last look at the rare shark as it surfaced and then dove out of sight.

That afternoon in 1991 off the tip of Baja California was the most rewarding experience of her career.

Nicknamed the Shark Lady, Genie spent more than seven decades studying "magnificent, misunderstood" sharks. Her innovative research debunked common myths about many of the 350 shark species that had been stereotyped as vicious deep-sea thugs or brainless eating machines. She also investigated a wide variety of other amazing sea creatures around the globe.

Genie's love of the ocean and its creatures started when she was a young child. Fascination, curiosity, and courage never left her—even when she met with difficult obstacles pursuing her career as a female, mixed-race marine biologist and ichthyologist (fish expert) at a time when the field was dominated almost exclusively by white men.

Genie Clark was born May 4, 1922, in New York City. Her mother, Yumico Mitomi, was Japanese. Her American father, Charles Clark, died when she was a baby. To make ends meet, her mother often had to work long hours selling newspapers and other items in the lobby of a New York club.

When Genie was nine years old, her mother took her to the New York Aquarium that once stood at the southern tip of Manhattan. Spellbound, she leaned over a brass railing and brought her face as close as possible to an enormous tank filled with green water and mysterious, undulating creatures. "I pretended I was walking on the bottom of the sea," she later wrote.

Every Saturday while her mother worked, Genie roamed the aquarium and studied the fish—from fast gliders to sluggish bottom creepers. On her birthday her mother splurged and bought Genie a 15-gallon aquarium complete with aquatic plants and gravel to serve as a home for the girl's growing collection of guppies, swordtails, and clown fish. Soon their three-room apartment turned into a menagerie that included salamanders, a horned toad, an alligator—even a black racer snake she named Rufus. From then on, every bit of Genie's allowance went toward the purchase of more creatures and supplies and food for them.

The ocean had captivated Genie since she was a toddler. On family expeditions to the beach on Long Island in the summer, she went swimming with her mother, grandmother, and uncle. Her mother was a strong, graceful swimmer even in rough surf. (One of her swimming secrets: softened chewing gum stuffed inside ears prevented swimmer's ear infections). The best swimmers, Genie soon realized, were the fish. How did they do it? She read every book she could find to discover their secrets.

Zoology, the study of animals, intrigued Genie throughout high school. How would she be able to afford college to pursue this interest? Luckily, she was accepted at tuition-free Hunter College, a women's college that was part of the New York City college system. She finished her degree in 1942, just as the United States entered World War II after Japan's attack on Pearl Harbor, Hawaii. This was an anxious time for Japanese-speaking American citizens, who were sometimes considered to be possible enemies.

Because of her Anglicized name and her background in science, Genie was able to find a job in a booming war industry—plastics. She worked 50 hours a week during the day at the factory and went to school at New York University at night to get her master's degree. The American Museum of Natural History was the site of her favorite classes about fishes. In 1947, she saw the vast Pacific Ocean and amazing sharks for the first time as a research assistant in animal behavior for the Scripps Institution of Oceanography in La Jolla, California. At Scripps she had her first chance to try diving—an experience that almost ended in tragedy. Old-fashioned equipment was heavy and cumbersome. Genie strapped on a large diving helmet with a face mask attached to a long hose that was connected to an air pump. She had trouble breathing on the sea floor and almost fainted before someone on the dive boat had the presence of mind to haul her up. The hose had kinked and her oxygen was cut off. Genie did not let this terrifying experience deter her. She rested, repaired the hose, and dove again.

Later that same year she had an opportunity to do research in the Philippines as the only woman scientist to work on a project surveying animal behavior. When she reached Hawaii, however, agents from the Federal Bureau of Investigation (FBI) stopped her for questioning because of her Japanese ancestry. By the time the investigation ended, her

Genie Clark examines a bull shark near the coast of the Yucatan Peninsula in the Gulf of Mexico.

job had been given to a man. Two years later she returned to the South Pacific to collect fish in waters around the Marshall Islands, the Palaus, the Northern Marianas, and other territories that the United Nations had granted the United States to administer after World War II. The Office of Naval Research wanted to know which fish were poisonous. She found her best teachers among the most accomplished fishermen of Koror, Kwajalein, Guam, Saipan, and the Palaus. Native fishermen taught her how to use a spear to retrieve examples.

Genie had hoped to attend Columbia University for her doctoral studies, but a scientist there reportedly told her, "If you do finish, you will probably get married, have a bunch of kids, and never do anything in science after we have invested our time and money in you." As if to prove this skeptic

In 1951 Genie Clark made the first of many trips to study fish in the Red Sea and later became a champion for conservation for this unique habitat.

wrong, she finished her Ph.D. in zoology in 1950 at New York University.

The next year she was awarded a Fulbright scholarship to go to the Red Sea—one of the saltiest, warmest, least spoiled bodies of water on earth—to study native fish. She returned to this amazing body of water dozens of times to study everything from sea anemones and clown fish to eels and pipefish. She wrote about her experiences in a best-selling book, *Lady with a Spear*, which was published in 1953.

During this busy period of her life, Clark married a young Greek-born doctor, Ilias Papakonstantinou, who shared her love of the sea. She and Papakonstantinou returned to New York City. She started a job with the Museum of Natural History. Meanwhile, *Lady with a Spear*, which reflected her vivid enthusiasm for the ocean, created new op-

portunities for her and her family. The book inspired a job offer from a wealthy couple, William H. and Anne Vanderbilt, who owned property on Florida's west coast. They wanted to build a marine biology laboratory. In 1954, they asked Genie to be its director.

She moved south with her husband, toddler Hera, who had been born in 1952, and a newborn, Aya. Genie gave birth to a total of four children between 1952 and 1958. The children would all learn to swim before they learned to walk. When they grew older, they joined Genie on research expeditions and became accomplished divers. Genie even shared her passions with her grandchildren. Her grandson, Eli Weiss, recalled, "She took me swimming with whale sharks in Mexico when I was very young."

Cape Haze Laboratory started out as a small wooden outbuilding with shelves, a dock with a boat, and one employee, who was a seasoned fisherman. Genie was excited to have a chance to study the little-known sea life of the Gulf of Mexico. Living sharks became the focus of her research, which examined how lemon sharks think and learn.

Genie trained two nine-foot lemon sharks that lived in a shark pen. At feeding time she lowered a target into the pen. Fish dangled from a string. To get the fish, the shark had to hit the target just right, which set off a bell. Soon the sharks associated the sound with food. She kept changing the sharks' tasks to make the test harder. Each time the sharks displayed their skills. One female shark discovered that if she waited in the feeding area for a male to punch the target with its nose, she could grab the fish reward before he did.

During the next twelve years at Cape Haze, her research showed that sharks were more intelligent than anyone suspected. While she did not deny that great white sharks and tiger sharks can be dangerous to humans, especially when provoked, she insisted that the majority of sharks are not man-eating. "You have a better chance of being hit by a car when you leave your house than [of] being attacked by a shark when you go swimming."

New buildings were added to Cape Haze as visitors and researchers grew in number. In 1960, the laboratory moved to Siesta Key in Sarasota, Florida. Seven years later, Genie's marriage ended.

In 1967, she started teaching marine biology at the University of Maryland, where she worked until her retirement in 1992. The growing laboratory in Florida was turned over to a new director and a new sponsor. Mote Marine Laboratory and Aquarium became its new name.

During the next four decades, Genie completed more than 200 field research expeditions all over the world, from Papua

While diving off the coast of the Izu Peninsula, Japan, Genie Clark examined a giant Japanese spider crab, a deep-sea creature with a claw span of 12 feet.

★ 5 ★

New Guinea to the Cayman Islands. She led 72 dives using high-tech submersibles, small one- to three-person submarines that probe the ocean's deepest, darkest, unknown territory thousands of feet below the surface. Once, while searching for a giant six-gill shark 2,000 feet down, her submersible became wedged under a rock cliff ledge. "I was alarmed," she later said, "but not really afraid." Hours later, cold, tired, and damp, she and her crew finally managed to free the craft.

One of her most dangerous research missions probed narrow underwater caves off the coast of Mexico's Yucatán Peninsula. During 99 dives, she and her team of researchers entered cramped spaces filled with dozens of requiem sharks that were 2 to 18 feet in length. The ordinarily active and occasionally deadly creatures seemed to be "sleeping." They were

While doing research in the Red Sea, Genie Clark discovered the first effective shark repellent in the secretions of this flat fish called Moses sole.

breathing but did not move or attack. Why?

Genie and her team had to work quickly and carefully to examine the lethargic sharks crowded into a corner in the back of the cave. If the creatures awoke, they'd attack. In spite of the danger, Genie was thrilled for the opportunity to be face-to-face with the remarkable creatures. "It was an unforgettable moment in my life," she later wrote.

Genie's team, which included her grown-up daughter, Aya, used instruments to measure the cave's water temperature, current, carbon dioxide content, and salinity (salt concentration). They found that the water in the cave seemed to have a higher oxygen level and lower salt content, perhaps because of nearby freshwater underground springs. Genie later described these caves as possible soothing "cleaning stations" for the sharks. Annoying parasites appear to release their grip from the sharks' skin in these water conditions. Small remora fish then finish the cleanup.

Throughout her life, Genie worked hard to mentor and inspire women and minorities to become the next generation of marine biologists. "I never let being a woman—even as a young girl—stop me from trying to do something I really wanted to do, especially if it concerned fishes or the underwater world," she said in 2009. Genie's daughter Aya Konstantinou followed her mother's advice and became a pilot for a major airline. "She gave me the ability to believe I could do whatever I wanted to." Dr. Sylvia Earle, an American oceanographer born in 1933, described

Genie Clark was an avid diver all her life. Pictured here in 2005 at age 83, she made her last dive in 2014 while studying deep water triggerfish in the Solomon Islands. She was 92.

group of researchers in 2014 off the coast of the Solomon Islands to study triggerfish. Once she was in the water, one observer noted, "her buoyancy control was perfect. The minute she was underwater she was in her twenties again." When asked if this was her last dive, feisty Genie replied, "You're so pessimistic."

Her last research project, a study of mysterious deepwater triggerfish in the Solomon Islands and Thailand, was published just weeks before she died, February 25, 2015, age 92, of complications from non-smoking-related lung cancer.

Genie as an "intrepid leader, explorer, scientist, teacher, communicator, and friend." Like Genie's, Sylvia's achievements are remarkable. She has led more than a hundred expeditions and logged more than 7,000 hours underwater, including leading the first team of women aquanauts in 1970.

Genie, who wrote more than 175 scholarly and popular scientific articles and narrated several shark film and television documentaries, remained a lifelong champion for ocean conservation. Along with other environmental advocates, she helped persuade the Egyptian government in 1983 to create its first national park among the spectacular coral reefs of Ras Mohammad in the Red Sea in 1983.

92-year-old Genie made a dive with a

CHAPTER TWO

Gertrude Elion

At six-thirty in the morning on October 17, 1988, 70-year-old Gertrude "Trudy" Elion received a shocking phone call at her home in North Carolina. "Congratulations! You've won the Nobel Prize," an unfamiliar voice said.

Was this some kind of prank? "Quit your kidding," Trudy replied. "I don't think it's funny." As soon as she hung up, another reporter called. How did she feel about sharing the Nobel Prize in Physiology or Medicine with Dr. George Hitchings, her former boss and coworker from Burroughs Wellcome Company, and Sir James W. Black of the University of London? What was it like to be one of only five women in the 87 years of its history to have ever won a Nobel Prize in science or physiology?

Interviewers kept her phone line busy all day. With characteristic down-to-earth humor, Trudy recalled, "I never finished dressing, before there was a reporter at the door from a local newspaper, and I'm trying to answer the phone and trying to comb my hair, and the photographer is taking pictures," she said, and laughed. "Some of those pictures are really weird."

It turned out that the Nobel Prize Committee had issued a press release announcing that Trudy had won the Nobel Prize with Dr. Hitchings and Sir James Black at noon in Stockholm, Sweden, which was six o'clock in the morning on the East Coast of the United States. Trudy had been so busy answering calls, the Nobel Committee couldn't get through to tell her the good news that the three of them had been awarded the prize "for their discovery of important principles for drug treatment." The winners were to share $390,000 and the prestigious award, the first Nobel for drug research in 31 years.

Trudy and Hitchings were being honored for demonstrating the differences in nucleic acid metabolism between normal cells and disease-causing cancer cells, protozoa, bacteria, and viruses. They received special praise for their "more rational approach based on the understanding of basic biochemical and physiological processes." Instead of traditional trial and error methods, they had used

Trudy Elion, 73, received the National Medal of Science and was honored as the first woman elected to the Inventors Hall of Fame in 1991.

a revolutionary approach. By examining small differences between how normal and abnormal cells reproduce, they discovered ways to create drugs that eliminated specific unhealthy cells. The resulting drugs helped countless individuals suffering from malaria, gout, leukemia, or herpes viruses. One treatment assisted in successful organ transplant operations.

Trudy did not fit the mold for a typical Nobel Prize laureate. She had no doctorate degree. Retired since 1983, she was being given the award for a lifetime of work. And she was a woman. To celebrate her pathbreaking award, Trudy took her entire family (including four great nieces and nephews under age four) to Stockholm for the ceremony, which was attended by the king of Sweden, Carl XVI Gustaf, and dozens of world-famous scientists.

Trudy Elion's long and remarkable 39-year career in biochemistry at Burroughs Wellcome began when she was hired as a research assistant by Dr. George Hitchings, pictured here in 1948.

"Everybody said, 'How does it feel to get the Nobel Prize?' And I said, 'It's very nice but that's not what it's all about.'" For Trudy the real reward was always helping patients. "What greater joy can you have than to know what an impact your work has had on people's lives?"

Trudy never thought of a scientist as someone who wore a white lab coat and hid from the world among beakers and microscopes. Her mission throughout her life was to discover cures for people suffering from diseases. One of her most precious awards was the simplest: a heartfelt letter from a woman who enclosed her teenage daughter's photo.

My daughter Tiffany was stricken with herpes encephalitis in September, 1987. A neurologist said the only hope for her was possibly the drug acyclovir. I have thanked the Lord so many times that he blessed you with

the determination, stamina, love, and patience to work all of the long hours, days, months, and years it takes to invent a new drug. Tiffany is a senior in high school this year and doing great. May the Lord bless you beyond your wildest dreams.

Trudy was from an immigrant family who dreamed big. She was born in New York City on January 23, 1918. Her parents were teenage Jewish immigrants from Eastern Europe who came alone to the United States. Her Lithuanian father, Robert, managed to put himself through dental school. He built up a sizable practice and invested in real estate. Her "self-effacing, gentle" mother, Bertha, came from what is now Poland. She married at 19 and did not finish her education. However, she always supported her daughter's academic interests and advised Trudy to have a career so she could have her own money.

Another important person in Trudy's life was her Russian grandfather, who came to live with the family when she was three. A learned biblical scholar, he knew many languages and was a watchmaker until his eyesight failed. Trudy enjoyed their trips to the park and listening to his Yiddish stories. A fiery redhead, Trudy was a shy bookworm who loved school. She recalled enjoying Paul de Kruif's *Microbe Hunters*. When she was six, her brother Herbert was born and the family moved to the Bronx, which seemed like wide-open country to her.

The Elions' savings vanished in 1929, when the stock market crashed and Robert Elion lost all of his investments. He would spend the rest of his life struggling to repay his creditors. Trudy graduated early from high school with honors but did not know how she would be able to afford college. In spite of fierce academic competition, she was accepted at Hunter College, the free, all-woman's college that was part of the city college system of New York.

When Trudy was 15 and about to start college, tragedy struck. Her beloved grandfather was dying of stomach cancer, and she felt very helpless when she visited him at the hospital. "Suddenly, it came to me that maybe there was something I could do about cancer, that maybe I could become a scientist," she recalled. "I don't think I anticipated the trouble that was awaiting me. But I was determined to try anyway and having made my decision, I never wavered."

Her father encouraged her to study den-tistry or medicine, but Trudy Elion had other ideas. She chose chemistry because she did not want to take biology and have to dissect frogs. Her grandfather's death in 1933 continued to haunt her. Her quest was to find a cure for cancer.

In 1937, in the midst of the Great Depression, Trudy graduated with highest honors, but she had no idea where she would find work with a degree in chemistry. The jobs that existed were given to men. She applied for fellowships at 15 graduate schools to continue her studies in chemistry. Again she was turned down because she was a woman. When she finally did get an interview for a job working in a laboratory, she was told she was qualified, but they'd never hired a woman before because women were "too distracting."

"I almost fell apart," remembered Trudy. "That was the first time that I thought being a woman was a real disadvantage. It surprises me to this day that I didn't get angry. I got very discouraged."

Around this time she became engaged to be married to a statistics major from City College of New York. Unfortunately, he got sick with acute bacterial endocarditis, a strep infection of the heart valves and lining, and he died. This infection could have been cured a few years later with the discovery of penicillin. Trudy was heartbroken, and she never married. Later she said that the death reinforced in her mind the importance of scientific discovery. "It really was a matter of life and death to find treatments of diseases that hadn't been cured before."

For the next several years she cobbled together what jobs she could. She signed up for secretarial school and taught biochemistry to nursing students and high school students. She was living at home, trying to save money to go back to graduate school. While she was at a party, she met a chemist and offered to work for him for free so that she could learn how to operate equipment. "Even when I couldn't find a job, [my parents] supported me financially and never suggested that I should abandon my goals or get married. They never made me feel that I wasn't welcome to stay as long as I wanted. Without their support, I would have been unable to continue."

Hard work, devotion, and persistence were essential. Trudy was able to save money she made as a doctor's office receptionist. She finished her graduate studies in chemistry at night in 1941 at New York University. When the United States entered World War II in 1942, the number of men in chemistry labs dwindled as they were drafted or enlisted to fight overseas. "No question in my mind that I might never have gotten a research job if it hadn't been for World War II," she said. "Jobs were finally open to women."

Her first paid lab job wasn't glamorous, but she learned all she could working in quality control at a grocery store chain. She measured the color of mayonnaise and tested the acidity of pickles.

The big plus for her was learning about laboratory instrumentation. When she learned all she could, she quit. In 1944, she was hired in a lab at Johnson & Johnson in New Jersey, where she synthesized drugs called sulfonamides that help cure infections. This job lasted only six months. She was offered another position testing the strength of sutures, but she replied, "I don't think that is what I want to do, thank you very much."

A chance remark by her father and what turned out to be pure luck changed everything. He had noticed the Burroughs Wellcome Company name on a bottle of Empirin painkiller at his dentistry office. He told her that the company was only eight miles from their house. "Why not get an interview?"

Even though it was Saturday, Trudy put on her best hat and gloves and went to the laboratory, a converted rubber factory in Tuckahoe, New York. (The war effort kept many

Trudy Elion stood out as one of the few women laureates at the December 1988 Nobel ceremony in Stockholm, Sweden.

manufacturers open on weekends.) Fortunately, George Hitchings, who worked every other weekend, was in the lab. The laconic researcher had already hired one woman and did not seem to exhibit the prejudice against women that Trudy had experienced at other jobs. Trudy's verve and impressive academic résumé, he later said, impressed him. However, the only other female employee thought Trudy seemed "too elegant." Trudy could tell. "She looked at me," Trudy remembered, "and said, 'She's no chemist. She won't get her hands dirty.'"

Hitchings hired Trudy as a lab assistant for $50 a week. She started work June 14, 1944, and stayed at Burroughs Wellcome for the next 39 years. The company was unusual. A pharmaceutical operation started in England, it was set up as a trust to let researchers discover drugs without the usual profit-driven bottom line. The lab department was small—another plus. There were only two other employees besides Trudy.

Hitchings was interested not only in drug development but how the medical community was conducting research. While every other pharmaceutical company was using trial and error to come up with new drugs, Hitchings thought this was inefficient. Why not use a rational, scientific method? He wanted to find out how normal and abnormal cells reproduced and to develop drugs to interrupt the life cycle of abnormal cells while leaving healthy cells unharmed. To do this he compared how cells grew and changed as they were exposed to different drugs. He suggested to Trudy that she investigate little-known components of nucleic acids (also called RNA and DNA). She explored building blocks of nucleic acids called purine bases, which help transmit hereditary data to cells. She explained, "I loved the job because I was allowed to advance at my own rate. I could do as much as I wanted to do." She stayed late and showed up on weekends, even though the conditions were awful. (The temperature on the lab floor could be 140 degrees because of a baby food factory on the floor below.) She didn't care. At Burroughs Wellcome there were no barriers to her leaping into related scientific fields—wherever her insatiable curiosity took her. Other places would have told her, "This is as far as you can go. You're a chemist. Why do you want to be an immunologist? Why are you interested in virology?"

Meanwhile Trudy commuted to school after work for two years to get her Ph.D. One day the Brooklyn Polytechnic Institute told her she had to quit her job and go to graduate school full-time. This posed a hard choice for Trudy. She wanted a Ph.D. as a credential, yet she knew she'd never find another job like the one she had. She told the school that she couldn't stop working. Trudy's drive to experiment and find cures for diseases was spurred on by the death in 1956 of her beloved mother, who had cervical cancer.

Full of determination, she used the discovery of one compound as a tool to find another. Soon Trudy began publishing technical papers based on her research. Hitchings said she could include her name as author, which was another enlightened act for the time. Eventually she published 225 papers. Her work fascinated her. She shared data she discovered and went to conferences to make presentations and discuss the latest research with other scientists.

Her work with Hitchings, she said, was "an evolution." In the beginning she was one of three assistants in the department. "He told me what he wanted done, and it was up to me to determine the best way to proceed, and then do it." Hitchings and Trudy discovered drugs that made organ transplants possible. They found a drug that transformed childhood leukemia from a disease that was almost always fatal to an illness that 80 percent of victims survive.

As she proved herself more and more capable, Hitchings gave her more autonomy, and eventually she was given assistants from related fields such as biochemistry and pharmacology. "Pretty soon I had a good-sized group that grew as the department grew." Hitchings became a vice president. After 23 years with the company, she was finally made head of the Department of Experimental Therapy, a department she had created.

One of her department's landmark breakthroughs came in 1977, after four years of nonstop, grueling research. "I had the most wonderful group of young people working together," Trudy recalled. "If ever there was a team effort, that was the one."

Under her direction they had analyzed, tested, and investigated the drug acyclovir to find out how it worked. Reports from the early 1970s had shown that this drug was active against two kinds of viruses, tiny organisms that latch onto healthy cells in order to grow and then multiply out of control, causing a wide range of diseases with no known cure. The viruses, known as herpes simplex and herpes zoster, cause mild diseases such as cold sores and chicken pox. They can also cause more serious illnesses by making people blind, infecting the brain, and causing death.

Up until this point, antiviral drugs were considered too risky and toxic because they attacked both the virus *and* the healthy cell. "Those of us who started in antiviral chemotherapy . . . were considered a little crazy," Trudy later wrote.

Did she care? Not a bit. She knew she was on the right track, drawing upon a hunch that led her back to research she'd done 30 years earlier. All science, she said, is a continuation of science that went before. A good scientist never ignores unexpected results and learns from her mistakes. The best scientific ideas, she said, "are the result of trying to figure something out that puzzles you. You constantly are thinking over the results and asking, 'What does it mean?' and 'Why did it happen?'"

Their persistence paid off. That afternoon in 1977, Trudy and her eclectic team of chemists, biochemists, virologists, and oncologists set up an experiment exposing acyclovir to virus-infected cells and noninfected cells. Both batches were incubated for seven hours. Special equipment analyzed the extracts. Results showed that the drug targeted the infected cells and not the healthy ones.

After fine-tuning the drug further, they figured out that acyclovir had tricked the virus into absorbing a compound that killed it. "At first no one believed it possible," she said. "Everybody was very excited."

Working in secrecy, the team finally unveiled the new drug at a conference in 1978. The discovery was viewed as a major breakthrough. Eight years later, the Food and Drug Administration (FDA) gave its approval for distribution to the public. The drug quickly became Burroughs Wellcome's single most profitable product. The success of acyclovir helped lay the critical foundation for research by the same group she had trained. After Trudy's retirement in 1983, her team's work resulted in the discovery of AZT, the only drug approved by the FDA for patients with AIDS.

In retirement, Trudy pursued her great love of travel and opera while continuing at Burroughs Wellcome as emeritus researcher. She enjoyed teaching research methods to medical students at Duke University. "It's a wonderful life," she wrote, "I don't think I could have chosen anything that would have made me happier." She worked hard to promote and mentor women in the field of chemistry. When she was awarded $250,000 by Burroughs Wellcome to donate to charity, she gave the prize money to the college she attended to fund fellowships for women in chemistry and biochemistry. "I think women must have the confidence to pursue their goals without the fear that they cannot succeed," she said in an interview.

She helped further the careers of two generations of scientists, always challenging them and trying to make sure there was a good rationale for their science. She asked the young scientists hard questions. "If we carry out these experiments," she said, "how will we use the information generated, and where will this lead us?"

Honors poured in for Trudy, who had become a highly visible role model for women after winning the Nobel Prize in 1988. She was awarded the National Medal of Science in 1991 and was elected to the National Academy of Sciences. With 45 patents to her name, she was the first woman to win a place in the National Inventors Hall of Fame. She also received 25 honorary doctorates. Her fame never went to her head. She remained approachable and willing to listen. "Every time I give a talk at a university or medical school, someone will come up to me afterwards and say, 'I want you to know that I've had a kidney transplant for twenty years thanks to your drug,' or 'My child who had leukemia is graduating from college.' There isn't anything that can give you greater satisfaction than that."

Trudy Elion died at home in her sleep in 1991, age 81.

CHAPTER THREE
Katherine Coleman Johnson

Of the millions of Americans who watched live television coverage of the dramatic liftoff of Project Mercury's *Freedom 7* at Cape Canaveral, Florida, at 9:30 EST on the morning of May 5, 1961, few may have been as anxious as Katherine Coleman Johnson. Her mathematical computations were about to help send American astronaut Alan B. Shepard Jr., into orbit around the Earth.

So much was riding on the mission's success.

The United States was in a neck and neck race for space with the Soviet Union (which inluded what is now called Russia and other nearby countries). Just three weeks earlier, Russian cosmonaut Yuri Gagarin had become the first man in space. Now the United States hoped to overtake the Russian space program's lead by sending its first manned spacecraft into orbit. Unlike Gagarin, Shepard would be able to maneuver the spacecraft himself. Would everything go as planned?

Nervously, 43-year-old Katherine watched as boosters roared beneath the seven-story-high, 66,000-pound Redstone rocket. The ground shook. Slowly, *Freedom 7* rose into the sky.

Dozens of variables—everything from speed and atmosphere resistance to gravitational pull and time—had been used to calculate the launch, trajectory, orbit, and return flight of the spacecraft. Before the invention of reliable electronic computers, the accuracy and safety of space flight depended on people like Katherine and the rest of the Langley Field Research team, who crunched numbers with slide rules and mechanical calculators. (The word "computer" was first used to describe the person who did the math—not the machine.) The math equations of Katherine and her team of "computers" were checked and rechecked countless times. There could be no errors.

Undoubtedly, Katherine breathed a sigh of relief when *Freedom 7* reached the predicted altitude of 116 miles above Earth,

In 1966 Katherine Coleman Johnson was one of a team of "computers" who did calculations with adding machines.

orbited 15 minutes and 28 seconds at a velocity of 5,134 miles per hour, and pulled a maximum of 11Gs. This meant that Shepard experienced 11 times the normal gravitation force that we feel on Earth. For five exciting minutes, Shepard also experienced weightlessness.

Flawlessly, Shepard maneuvered the capsule's descent through the Earth's atmosphere and splashed down safely in the Atlantic Ocean—exactly on target. A waiting aircraft carrier, the USS *Lake Champlain*, sent a helicopter to retrieve Shepard inside the capsule. The capsule was deemed in such good shape by inspecting engineers that it would be reused. Shepard, too, survived the ordeal with flying colors.

While Shepard experienced a hero's welcome, with a medal from President John F. Kennedy and parades in cities across the

All systems were go on May 5, 1961, when *Freedom 7* with astronaut Alan B. Shepard Jr. aboard successfully launched.

country, the behind-the-scenes NASA technicians, engineers, and scientists went largely uncelebrated. However, for Katherine, *Freedom 7* was a turning point in her life.

"I have always loved the idea of going into space. I still do," she said. She knew that she was on the ground floor of something important, something big. "The whole idea of going into space was new and daring. We were pioneers of the space era."

As an African American woman *and* a mathematician, she faced many obstacles working in a brand-new science agency that was still almost entirely white and entirely male, except for the clerical staff. When she arrived at Langley, black "computers" were assigned to a segregated office. Women—even those with expertise—were told they could not attend meetings. While men with

similar academic credentials were classified as "professionals," women were "sub professionals" and were paid substantially less. Women's names were not allowed on research reports they helped create.

Katherine's luck, determination, and talent were key to her success. In 1953, a few weeks after she was hired, she was "loaned" to the Flight Research Division, a top secret space project. This was her first big break. For the next three years she asked questions. Lots of questions. She wanted to learn about the science of aeronautics that the engineers and scientists were discussing behind closed doors. Finally, they let her attend the meetings. After much pushing and cajoling her coauthored report with the hefty title *Determination of Azimuth Angle at Burnout for Placing a Satellite over a Selected Earth Position* (1959) came out with her name on it. Before she retired in 1986, she coauthored 21 technical papers.

Her computations were used to help track the 1962 trajectories of astronaut John Glenn's orbit around the Earth and return. She assisted on the team that developed navigational tools that astronauts could use if their spacecraft lost contact with ground control or computers failed.

In preparation for the Apollo moon landing in 1969, she worked on the team that calculated the lunar orbit and landing of a spacecraft on the surface. Massive electronic computers located in California, across the country from Langley, were now being used extensively for calculations. However, they still weren't entirely trusted. What if they broke down? When a fuel tank exploded in 1970 on the Apollo 13 Mission en route to the moon, onboard computers malfunctioned on the spacecraft. Katherine was part of the team assembled to monitor the flight of the spacecraft, which made it back safely to Earth.

Nothing about her beginnings hinted that she would one day work in the high-tech field of space exploration. Katherine Coleman was born August 26, 1918, in the foothills of the Appalachian Mountains in the sleepy town of White Sulphur Springs, West Virginia. She was the youngest of the four children of Joshua McKinley Coleman and Joylette Coleman. Her father, who had a sixth-grade education, worked as a farmer and part-time laborer. Her mother was a former schoolteacher.

From an early age numbers fascinated Katherine. She loved to count. The steps to the road from her house. The steps up to the church. The number of dishes and silverware she washed. "Anything that could be counted, I did," she said. She was always eager to learn. She wanted to know everything she could about the world around her.

The past was very much alive in the river valleys, hollows, and rugged foothills of her West Virginia home. People in her small rural town recalled clearly the bloody battles of the War Between the States, commonly known as the Civil War, which raged from 1861 to 1865. The year before the war broke out, 490,380 slaves—almost a third of the

state's total population—lived in Virginia and West Virginia.

When Katherine was a young girl, White Sulphur Springs was home to many ex-slaves and children of ex-slaves. They told stories of the hard times before slavery was abolished in 1865, when people of color were purchased and sold like property to work on nearby farms in Greenbrier County. By law slaves had no constitutional rights. They could not testify in court against a white person, travel without permission, make a will, or own personal property. They could not marry without their master's consent. Teaching a slave to read or write was forbidden. Since they could be killed or sold with impunity, one of the greatest fears a slave faced was being separated from family and friends. Slaves were sold to other masters, rented out, used as prizes in raffles or wagers in card games and horse races.

As for so many African Americans in

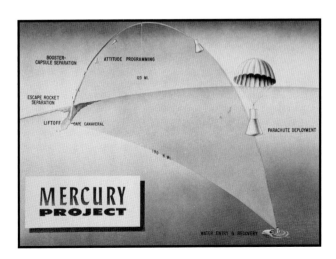

The first manned space mission for the United States, Project Mercury, depended on accurate mathematical calculations for lift-off, orbit, and reentry.

Right on target the *Freedom 7* capsule made an Atlantic Ocean landing and was retrieved by helicopter to be taken to aircraft carrier *Lake Champlain*.

White Sulphur Springs and the surrounding area, slavery cast a shadow on the Coleman family. They had lived in this part of the Appalachians as far back as 1799. Katherine's great-grandmother, Louisa Johnson, was 70 years old when she died of "paralysis" in 1869 in Jefferson County. Records show she was a servant or slave and her parents were "not known." Her daughter, Margaret Wheeler, may have led a very different life. Born in 1839 in Greenbrier County, Margaret was officially listed as "free colored," which meant she was not a slave. How or why she was freed was not recorded. She was one of only an estimated 3,000 freed slaves in West Virginia. Her freedom meant something important. By law her children were automatically free.

Margaret Wheeler's free status would ultimately have a profound effect on Katherine Johnson Coleman's father, Joshua McKinley Coleman. Although Joshua was born in 1881, after the 1865 passage of the Thirteenth Amendment to the U.S. Constitution abolishing slavery, he was listed in official records as a "free black male." His strong opinions about equality and freedom were passed on to his daughter, Katherine. "My dad taught us 'you are as good as anybody in this town, but you're no better,'" Johnson later said. "I don't have a feeling of inferiority. Never had. I'm as good as anybody, but no better."

Her father was one of the biggest influences in her life. He was determined that all four of his children would have the best education he could get for them, no matter the sacrifice.

In White Sulfur Springs during the first half of the twentieth century, where you went to school was determined by the color of your skin. Under segregation, white and black children were separated by law. The ramshackle schoolhouses for "colored children" offered classes only up to fifth or sixth grade and had poorly paid teachers and scant supplies. In all of West Virginia there were only two high schools and two colleges that admitted black students.

The color line was etched into other day-to-day aspects of life. The color of your skin determined where you could buy a sandwich, drink from a drinking fountain, or use a bathroom. "Coloreds only" and "whites only" were signs posted everywhere in White Sulphur Springs. The local posh hotel, Greenbrier Hotel, long viewed as the meeting place for the "best Southern society," did not allow African Americans until the mid-1950s. Hotel workers like Joshua McKinley Coleman had to use a special back entrance and were forbidden to talk to guests unless spoken to first.

Joshua Coleman decided to seek the best available education for his children. As soon as her eldest brother turned 14, Katherine and her family packed up their belongings in a wagon and traveled the rutted road across the open hill country, river valleys, and rugged hills west to Institute, West Virginia. For the next eight years, from September to May, the family lived in a rented house in Institute. While Katherine's mother worked as a domestic, her father returned to White Sulphur Springs to earn a living. "We only got to see my father about once a month during the school year. I know it was a real sacrifice for he and my mother—being separated like that for most of the year."

Institute was the home of West Virginia Collegiate Institute, which had been called West Virginia Colored Institute until 1891. The all-black school provided a high school education, vocational training, and teacher preparation. It was considered the center of black intellectual life in the state and featured well-respected faculty, many of whom had gone to colleges in the North.

Katherine entered the high school when she was only 10. Her teachers encouraged her to pursue mathematics. She worked with many wonderful mentors. She graduated from high school at age 15 and went on to earn a bachelor's degree in math and French in 1937. At that point the school had been renamed West Virginia State University and had grown to 1,000 students.

As soon as Katherine graduated she began working. She taught math and science in small, all-black schools in West Virginia and Virginia for the next 18 years. While teaching, she went back for graduate studies in math and physics at West Virginia State. In 1939 she married her first husband, James Goble. They had three daughters, Constance,

NASA mathematician Katherine Coleman Johnson's computations helped influence every major space program from Mercury through the Space Shuttle.

On November 24, 2015, Katherine Coleman Johnson was awarded the Presidential Medal of Freedom by President Barack Obama in the East Room of the White House in Washington, D.C.

Kathy, and Joylette. Joylette also became a mathematician.

When her husband died of brain cancer in 1956, Katherine went back to work part-time as a high school math teacher in Newport News, Virginia. She remarried in 1959. She took the name of her new husband, James Johnson.

In 1952, a relative mentioned that jobs were opening up at what was then the National Advisory Committee for Aeronautics (NACA), the predecessor of NASA. The jobs were open to African American women as "computers" at Langley Field Research Center in Virginia. Langley had been used during World War II to test fighter engines and perform research on aeronautics. The job seemed like a great opportunity. With her mathematics background, working six days a week, her starting salary was $1,662 per year. As a teacher in the rural South, she'd be lucky to make less than a third that amount.

"I had a wonderful, wonderful career at NASA," Katherine later said. Throughout her time at NASA, she reached out regularly to school groups and minority children to encourage them to pursue careers in math and science. She liked to advise students to go beyond the task at hand, ask questions, and be inquisitive. "Let yourself be heard," she said.

During her tenure at NASA Katherine received many awards, including the NASA Lunar Orbiter Award and three NASA Special Achievement Awards. She was named Mathematician of the Year in 1997 by the National Technical Association. In May 2016, on the fifty-fifth anniversary of Shepard's suborbital flight, NASA dedicated the Katherine G. Johnson Computational Research Facility at Langley Research Center. This 40,000-square-foot data center, which was named to honor Katherine's exceptional work, features cutting-edge technology that may one day help NASA send humans to Mars.

One of Katherine's proudest moments came in November 2015, when she was awarded the Presidential Medal of Freedom, the nation's highest civilian honor, by President Barack Obama. Receiving this honor from the first African American president of the United States seemed especially fitting for 97-year-old Johnson, who worked hard to overcome prejudice and promote the scientific work of women and minorities all her life.

CHAPTER FOUR
Marie Tharp

No one knew exactly what was hidden beneath the Atlantic Ocean until Marie Tharp went to work in the summer of 1952 plotting a detailed map of underwater mountains, valleys, ridges, and plains. Using sonar recordings of sea floor depths gathered by Lamont Geological Observatory scientists on research ships, she painstakingly created an image of what the ocean bottom might look like if someone pulled a giant plug and drained out all the water.

Marie noticed something strange as she moved her finger down her drawing of the mountain range that sprawled along the mid-Atlantic sea floor like the ridged spine and long tail of an alligator with its nose pointing to the north. A kind of crack seemed to run along the middle of the range. Excitedly, she checked and rechecked the sonar readings. Yes, it appeared to be a deep valley that followed the crest of the mountains.

Then she noticed something else. Some-

thing even more disturbing. Using another map that charted historical earthquake records, she discovered that a chain of seismic disturbances rocked this deep valley. The crack and the earthquake distribution matched.

Could this be evidence for continental drift—the controversial theory that massive landforms moved and shifted over time?

This notion was scientific heresy in the 1950s. "It was comparable to Copernicus saying that the sun, and not the Earth, was the center of the planetary system," Marie said. Scientists in the United States were convinced that the Earth's surface was static or unmoving.

When Marie showed the maps of the deep valley and earthquake records to her coworker Bruce Heezen, the geologist and oceanographer who had helped gather the sonar recordings on Atlantic research expeditions, he was "absolutely horrified." They

Marie Tharp at work in 1959. The sonar recordings she used to create stunning maps of the ocean floor are shown in rolls behind her and on the drawing table. The prototype of the globe she and Bruce Heezen created is by the window.

might both lose their jobs. Angrily, he called her wacky ideas nothing but "girl talk." It took hotheaded Marie a year to convince Heezen that she was right.

Marie's precise drafting showed new clues that seemed to indicate that perhaps there was a dynamic seam in the planet's crust, a kind of boundary where giant, continent-size plates shifted and shoved. This rift acted like a conveyor belt that caused continents to drift and move. Marie was among the first scientists to notice evidence for "plate tectonics," as this movement was later called.

For the next three decades she and Bruce worked as collaborators. He collected data at sea; she drew the maps, since women were not allowed to work on research ships until the late 1960s. The stunning charts they created have been called "the most remarkable achievements in modern cartography." In their own era, however, their views of the ocean floor ignited controversy that would turn geophysics upside down.

Mapmaking was in Marie's blood, she always liked to say. She was born July 30, 1920, in Ypsilanti, Michigan. Her father, William Edgar Tharp, who had finished only one year of high school, worked as a soil surveyor for the U.S. Department of Agriculture. "Papa," as she called him all her life, moved where his work took him from the Midwest to the East Coast, from the Appalachians to the Deep

South. He'd make borings of soils and chart contours of the land—hard, physical work.

As a child Marie loved to travel with him in his big green government truck. (She learned to drive when she was 11.) Her fondest memories were of tramping across the fields looking for arrowheads, "making mud pies and being a general nuisance." Her mother, Bertha Tharp, was a proper former schoolteacher—a much more shadowy figure in Marie Tharp's recollections.

The family moved so often that Marie never had much time to make friends. She always considered herself something of an outsider—an independent only child accustomed to spending time by herself. Early photographs show her red hair cut in a simple bowl cut; she wears sturdy overalls. Science did not interest her much in her early years, she said. Her mother tried to "civilize" her tomboy daughter with Sunday school and art lessons. When they lived in Washington, D.C., at various times, Marie enjoyed visiting the National Gallery and the Museum of Natural History.

By the time she reached high school, she had attended 18 different schools. The advantage of their constant movement meant that she had a chance to see many different landscapes. She first set eyes on the Atlantic Ocean when she was five or six. This was the time her father did mapping in Mobile County, Alabama. The beach and the constant movement of the waves amazed her.

Science did not intrigue Marie until she attended school in Florence, Alabama.

A teacher seemed to spark her talent. A few years later, her father retired and bought a run-down farm he intended to improve in rural Ohio. Before they had lived there a year, Bertha Tharp died. Marie was only 15. Later, she seldom spoke of her mother, her illness, or her own grief.

Marie decided to go to college at Ohio University. By the time she graduated in 1943, she said she had changed her major every semester. She had a hard time fitting into the college social scene. As she later explained, most people seemed to baffle her. Awkward and opinionated by turn, she struggled to fit in during the early 1940s when co-ed dress mandated conformity. Female students were expected to wear skirts of a certain length, anklets, saddle shoes, and high-neck sweaters with pearls. "Terrible" was the way she remembered the experience of having to look like someone she wasn't.

One thing Marie knew for sure. She did not want to graduate and take on the jobs available to women: secretary or nurse. "I couldn't type and I couldn't stand the sight of blood," she said. It seemed a relief when she finally discovered that she was good at drafting and geology. By the time she graduated, World War II had begun and she discovered from a notice on a bulletin board that if she completed a certain degree, she could get a job in a scientific area newly open to women: petroleum geology.

Marie attended classes at the University of Michigan to get her degree, and in 1945 traveled to Tulsa, Oklahoma, for a job as an assistant geologist with an oil company for the astronomical sum of two hundred dollars a month, twice what a teacher made. She was able to take advantage of science jobs that opened up because of the war. She worked at the oil company for three years and meanwhile earned another master's degree. However, she hated the work. "Not too challenging," she wrote of her experience. "Nothing to do. Hot."

In 1946, Marie married a violinist named David Flanagan, whom she'd met in Ohio. He had served in the U.S. Air Force during World War II. Before divorcing in 1952, they moved to New York City. Although she'd earned a bachelor's degree with a double major in English and music (with four minors) at Ohio University in 1943 and a master's degree in geology from the University of Michigan in 1944, and another in mathematics from the University of Tulsa in 1948, the best job she could find in New York City was working as a lowly research assistant to a group of male graduate students at Columbia University's Lamont Geological Observatory.

Beginning in 1949, Marie spent three years drafting simple maps and occasional diagrams and worked as a number cruncher, punching a primitive adding machine in the cramped geophysical lab. The data that she and the handful of other "human calculator" women in the department used included everything from underwater gravity and acoustics to seafloor depths and topography.

Although Marie had completed more academic training than most of her superiors, her job was strictly arithmetical—nothing theoretical, creative, or intellectually challenging. She became the frazzled go-to person in the department, the one depended

At Lamont's Oceanography building in the mid-1960s, Marie Tharp creates a physiographic diagram of the Indian Ocean. Sonar recordings are shown near her right elbow.

upon to create last-minute slides for conferences, collect maps, do odd carpentry jobs, make coffee, collate presentation booklets, and arrange data for an ever-growing group of demanding male researchers. She would never be granted permission to step aboard a research ship or think of original research or run her own lab. What she longed to discover, she later said, was "something I was good at, something I could get paid for, and something I really liked." What she wanted, she said, was "a once-in-the-history-of-the-world opportunity."

In the summer of 1952 Marie's luck finally changed when Bruce Heezen knocked on her office door carrying a cardboard box stuffed with rolls of paper. Bruce was a hulking, Iowa-born graduate student who was generally considered the "golden boy" and protégé of Lamont's brilliant, autocratic director, Dr. Maurice Ewing. The box he carried into Marie's office was filled with something she immediately recognized: fathometer records or echo soundings—sonar measurements of ocean depths made using echo sounders. The long scrolls of paper contained wavering lines that showed changes in the ocean floor terrain. Bruce had collected the echo soundings using recorders that continuously picked up signals as his research ship crisscrossed parts of the Atlantic Ocean during the past two years. Could she use these to make a map?

This was just the kind of once-in-the-history-of-the-world opportunity fierce, red-headed Marie had been waiting for. She went

Marie Tharp arrived in New York City in 1948. She applied for a job with Dr. Maurice "Doc" Ewing as a research assistant in his geophysical lab at Columbia University.

immediately to work on what soon proved to be an enormous task: translating 3,000 feet of echo sounding records into one drawing. Throughout the process Marie had to use patience, determination, and a rigorous kind of creativity. Often she had to intuit the lay of the land beneath the mysterious ocean where sonar records, which looked like the spikes, dips, and flat lines of recorded heartbeats, were missing.

Among her many talents (unknown at this point to her coworkers at Lamont) was her remarkable ability to think spatially—to imagine three-dimensional objects in space based on two-dimensional records. Even more importantly, she knew how to transfer this kind of visual representation onto paper so that other people could understand it as well.

In the years that followed, Marie's career and her social life would center around Lamont, where the base of operations had been moved from New York City to the Lamont Geological Observatory (now the Lamont-Doherty Earth Observatory) in Palisades, New York. The sprawling compound of buildings had been the estate of a philanthropic couple. In this more homelike setting, the people Marie worked with quickly became a kind of family to her. Her relationship with Bruce grew from friendship into a kind of lasting partnership, although they never married.

Lamont, however, did not remain a happy home. The evidence from Marie's maps of the ocean floor set off a firefight from the top. Each member of the department began to take sides. Continental drift was taboo since their boss, Dr. Ewing, was a

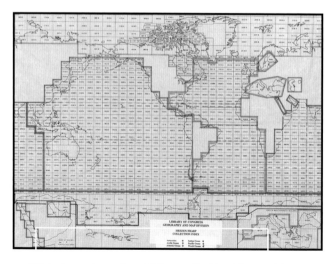

This bathymetric map from 1957 created by Marie Tharp and Bruce Heezen utilized maps, drawings, earth science data, and precision depth recordings gathered on research cruises.

"non-drifter." This period of their life Marie later called "the harassment." Bruce and Marie's working lives became increasingly difficult. Because of the heretical views that their work now showed, Dr. Ewing cut off their funding. He did what he could to thwart the map project, eventually forbidding Bruce from sailing on Lamont research vessels. They were not allowed to see collected data, but graduate students slipped them what they needed secretly.

Before Marie and Bruce were officially fired in 1968, she continued doggedly working on map projects at her Nyack, New York, home. These included freelance work she was doing for the U.S. Navy's National Ocean Survey, a four-year project that gave her a badly needed regular paycheck. Fortunately, there was other work as well. An earlier connection existed between *National Geographic*, staff at Lamont, and Dr. Ewing, who had written several articles for the popular magazine. Marie and Bruce were hired as freelance consultants by *National Geographic*.

In October 1967, *National Geographic* published a magnificent supplemental ocean floor map of the Indian Ocean, a physiographic diagram created by Marie and Bruce and painted in full color by Austrian landscape painter Heinrich Berann. Berann teamed up with them again to create the amazing "Atlantic Ocean Panorama," the ocean floor depiction created by Marie and Bruce. Marie traveled back and forth to Austria to work with Heinrich Berann and his assistant. As Marie liked to say, "*National Geographic* made

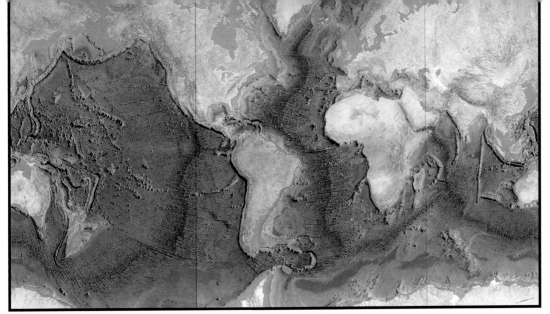

This World Ocean Floor Panorama map painted by Heinrich C. Berann, 1977, was created after more than two decades of work by Marie Tharp and Bruce Heezen.

us famous." Their last project for *National Geographic* concerned the area around Antarctica. It was published in 1975 in the National Geographic Society's *Atlas of the World*.

Meanwhile, Marie and Bruce had already begun a kind of masterpiece together: the World Ocean Floor map, published as the first comprehensive look at the ocean floors around the globe. The breathtaking painting, based on Marie's pen drawings of valleys and rifts, was also completed by Heinrich Berann. The map was painted on a six-and-a-half-foot-wide by four-feet-tall canvas. It shows a continuous, 40,000-mile-long seam running across the world's surface. This splendid global ocean map was funded by the U.S. Office of Naval Research.

In 1977, the year that the World Ocean Map was to be published, 53-year-old Bruce was invited to travel on a secret nuclear research submarine called the NR-1 to view firsthand the underwater world he'd spent so much time recording from above the waterline in ships.

On June 21, 1977, Marie set sail on the *Discovery*, a research ship that left from Barry, Wales, in a calm sea. She and Bruce were supposed to meet at Reykjavik, Iceland, to view a rift valley together by plane. Their trip never took place.

Bruce, who had the map manuscript with him, died suddenly of a heart attack while sailing off the coast of Iceland. Marie was shocked and heartbroken. Her long-time partner left her half of his possessions and his house. The other half went to his mother.

The loss of her beloved companion and collaborator was terrible for Marie. It took her several years to figure out what to do next. She continued to work on map projects with volunteers using data that Bruce had collected. She began organizing his files, which were given to the Geography and Map Division of the Library of Congress. The mountains of maps, correspondence, photos, and other data have taken years to be catalogued.

Only in later years was Marie finally given credit for her amazing work. In 1978, the National Geographic Society's Hubbard Medal was given to Marie Tharp, then 58, and Bruce Heezen. In 1996, the Society of Women Geographers presented Marie with its Outstanding Achievement Award. Although she had no source of steady income, Marie persevered and continued organizing Bruce's voluminous data and papers. She tried to support herself with freelance projects and her own mapmaking business. Always resourceful, she also rented out rooms of the house she'd inherited from Bruce.

Marie Tharp, like many other women scientists, was not allowed aboard research ships until the late 1960s.

Marie remained an avid gardener who was known to decorate her snow-covered yard with artificial flowers in the middle of winter. An enthusiastic cook, she loved to feed her friends and coworkers, many of whom helped her with her projects without pay. She had her own sense of culinary experimenting ("Chicken Jell-O anyone?"). She often made herself unique skirts created from old clothing that had belonged to her father or Bruce. She discovered Nike sneakers, abandoned her clunky black orthopedic shoes, and in her old age was partial to purple eyeliner, red lipstick, and nail polish with glitter.

In 1997, the Library of Congress hosted a special celebration honoring Marie with an important award from the Geography and Map Division's Philip Lee Phillips Society. She was honored as "one of the four greatest cartographers of the twentieth century." Later, she was especially moved when she was escorted in her wheelchair to take part in the Library's hundredth anniversary of the ren-ovated Jefferson Building. A special feature was the exhibit *American Treasures from the Library of Congress*.

Among the displays, which included Lewis and Clark's journals, was one of her maps of the ocean floor. When she saw this, she burst into tears. "How did it all happen?" she asked in a soft voice. Later, she turned to one of the Library of Congress staffers and said, "I wish that Papa and Bruce could see it."

After several years of declining health, Marie died of lung cancer on August 23, 2006. An intensely private woman all her life, she passed away alone at night in her hospital room after her many visitors had gone.

CHAPTER FIVE
Florence Hawley Ellis

Time was running out on June 28, 1960. If Florence Hawley Ellis and her team of archaeologists did not locate a significant find soon, bulldozers would begin scheduled road building and destroy the site known as San Gabriel del Yungue near the Rio Grande River. To make matters worse, 100-degree heat scorched the rolling New Mexico landscape.

Florence tugged off the bandanna tied around her head, mopped her sweaty face, and scanned the arid terrain from atop the site's upper East Mound. For the past two summers she and her crew of 60 young women and men had been carefully using shovels and trowels to remove layer upon layer of often rock-hard soil. Every artifact discovered—bone, potsherd, or piece of carbonized firewood—had to be sifted from the dirt, sorted, and recorded inch by inch, foot by foot in a grid pattern.

Yet they still had not found the mother lode—definitive proof of the different peoples who were thought to have once lived here.

Again Florence scanned the flat expanse to the south. This time something caught her eye. A patch of morning glories, rippling in the wind as blue-purple and rare as open water. Three decades of directing excavations (and her abiding love of gardening) had taught Florence many things about reading the rugged Southwestern terrain. Buried carbon-rich artifacts sometimes changed surrounding soil chemistry and promoted growth of unusual plants.

The morning glory patch seemed worth a try. She sent three crew members there to open up two test trenches. Hours later the diggers' jubilant shouts told the news. They'd discovered the corner of a room's wall made of cobblestones, and on the floor a broken black-on-red bowl. "The movement of the young excavators into the newly opened

Florence Hawley Ellis in 1940, age 27, near Chaco Canyon, New Mexico.

territory," she later remembered, "was nothing less than a land rush."

Thanks to Florence's persistence, the excavation would continue. The San Juan Pueblo, who had originally allowed Florence to dig here, extended their permission—due largely to her respectful 30-year relationship with the Pueblo.

During the next two seasons, Florence and her crew uncovered living quarters and the foundation and floor of a destroyed Catholic church. Artifacts included everything from biscuit tins and a religious medal to a carved gun stock and altar candlesticks. Uncovering layers was like traveling in a time machine through history. Four different cultural groups had made this place their home. At the deepest level was evidence of early native people from before the year 1300; then came Spanish invaders of the late 1500s; and finally settlers and Pueblos who lived and died there from 1800 on. Each fragment, each artifact flickered with its own tale.

Throughout her life Florence noticed connections among details that most people overlooked. Like a determined detective, Florence analyzed everything from tree rings (dendrochronology) and pottery pigment residues to weaving patterns and petroglyph shapes. Her goal was to understand what life was like in the Southwest hundreds and thousands of years ago.

While Florence was trained as an archaeologist, she wore two other professional hats: anthropologist and ethnologist. What could be learned about possible past ways of life from native people still living in their ancestral homelands? She believed that archaeology, anthropology, and ethnology could work together to help create a deeper, more complex picture of the native people of the Southwest.

Many of Florence's academic contemporaries assumed that early native populations who created vast dwellings in spectacular places like Chaco Canyon and Mesa Verde simply "vanished" or became "extinct." She questioned whether some of the early artifacts such as petroglyphs, pottery, and weavings had ties to activities and beliefs still practiced by native people in the early twentieth century. With deep respect she collected information from Pueblo and Navajo elders about

art, stories, religious beliefs, customs, and social organization among New Mexico and Arizona Pueblo and Navajo peoples. During this process she began to notice historical evidence of drought and the ongoing perils of climate change—the origin of so much settlement instability in the Southwest—long before these terms became well-known.

The field of archaeology was anything but welcoming to women during the late 1920s when Florence began her career. Digs were considered "man's work"—dirty,

Florence Hawley Ellis (right) supervising an archaeological dig in New Mexico in 1964.

dangerous, backbreaking, and in remote places like steep mountainsides, deep canyons, or riverbeds. Crews camped out in tents, often during the hottest times of the year. Biting insects, venomous snakes, and marauding coyotes posed hardships. Food and water had to be carried in to campsites.

Women leaders of excavations were very rare. Most women who went into archaeology in the 1930s were part of husband-wife teams, not independent professionals. Few male archaeologists believed that crews—made up mostly of men—would take orders from a woman.

Florence did not let these obstacles stop her. She wanted to upend the stereotype that "field archaeologist" and "woman" did not go together. While proper American women of her day were seldom seen outdoors without a hat, gloves, a skirt, and nylon stockings, Florence had to be practical about her clothing. In the field she wore heavy jeans and modified her blue workman's shirt with a ruffled edge and embroidered ladybugs. She tied her brown hair with colorful yarn ties and fastened red bows on her practical canvas shoes. (As project director, she did not have to wear heavy leather boots.)

Inside the leather dig bag that accompanied her in the field were a variety of practical necessities that included:

A pair of knee pads
A whisk broom
A toothbrush, used to clean objects in the field
A pocketknife on a large binder ring
A spiral-bound notebook
A mechanical pencil
A no. 2 pencil; a no. 3 pencil
Insect repellent towelette
Insect bite medicine applicator
A first-aid gauze pad in wrapper
Adhesive bandages
Four loose rubber bands
A small wad of toilet paper
Two empty plastic bags
A length of string
A trowel
A hand compass
A carpenter's rule
A 10-power hand lens
An empty cigarette box (she recycled her
  containers to hold artifacts)

Florence was raised in boundless, open country under an unforgiving Western sky. This was also where she spent almost all of her career.

Her birthplace was Cananea, a copper-mining town in Sonora, Mexico, on September 17, 1906. Her mother, Amy May Roach Hawley, was born in Wisconsin and raised in California. Florence's mother worked in a one-room adobe schoolhouse in the brutal desert climate of Arizona before the advent of air-conditioning. Fred Graham Hawley, Florence's father, was chief chemist at a large copper mine with a violent history of strike-breaking.

On June 1, 1906, 5,360 Mexican workers

1930s view from the top of the cliff near Chetro Ketl, Chaco Canyon, shows the walls and great kiva.

at the mine in Cananea walked off the job demanding higher pay and better working conditions. (They were paid three and a half pesos per day, while the white Americans were paid five pesos.) Angry strikers took over the downtown. Fifty people were jailed. A posse of 275 uninvited Arizona Rangers roared across the border. By 1910, the unrest in Cananea spread throughout northern Mexico and helped start the Mexican Revolution.

It wasn't until 1913, when they heard rumors of dynamite planted behind their three-room frame house, that Florence's parents decided to take two suitcases packed for an emergency from beneath the bed and make their getaway with seven-year-old Florence and her three-year-old brother, Paul. The United States border was 40 miles away.

The Hawleys went to live with extended family in Los Angeles, a completely different environment from the rough-and-tumble mining town in Mexico. The Hawleys' six-month stay in California provided Florence with her first formal schooling. The family moved again when Fred Hawley found a new job as a chemist in the smelter operation of the local copper mining company in Miami, Arizona. The one-street copper boomtown had 1,395 people.

In Arizona, Florence contracted diphtheria, a dangerous bacterial infection. Fortunately she survived the disease, but then she came down with rheumatic fever, a heart

Florence Hawley Ellis, wearing her usual field outfit, supervises a student surveyor and excavator at the University of New Mexico dig at San Gabriel del Yungue in 1964 in northern New Mexico.

condition, and had to stay in bed for months. Her mother tutored her. The girl's isolation may have contributed to her acute ability to observe the world. When she finally recovered her health, Florence proved to be a quick learner. She graduated from eighth grade at age 12 and high school at age 16.

Florence and her family went on informal digs in the Miami area, picnic outings inspired by her father's abiding interest in archaeology. One exciting discovery that Florence uncovered was an intact, 600-year-old shallow bowl with holes punched along the edge. The plate-like object was 11 inches in diameter. When she looked closely at the red clay, Florence saw ancient fingerprints. What native person made this? When?

These were questions that fascinated Florence.

She decided to go to the University of Arizona. To avoid taking an American history class that required dreaded memorization of dates, she signed up for something new: an archaeology course. The only professor in the Anthropology Department, Byron Cummings, made the suggestion to Florence. Cummings, who became the university's president in 1927, was a respected professional in the field whose mentorship would have a profound influence on Florence's career. He taught her how to observe, excavate, and record findings. Cummings became a family friend and participated in several of the Hawley family's informal excavations in the Miami area.

Florence graduated with a major in English and a minor in archaeology in 1927. The following year she worked on her master's degree in archaeology at the University of Arizona. She wrote her thesis on ancient Arizona ceramics discovered in excavated sites near Miami. She separated the various pottery types and suggested connections with Mexican wares. Meanwhile, she and her father collaborated on the first chemical analyses of black pottery pigments. They found that the pigments contained carbon, carbon mineral, and manganese. Their pioneering work showed how pottery paint distinctions could provide another tool to figure out when and where the ceramics may have been created. Their findings became her thesis, the first of 300 scientific papers and four books she would publish during the next 50 years.

Her teaching career began in 1928 with an annual salary of $1500. 22-year-old Florence was almost the same age as her students in the fledgling Archaeology Department of

This Pinto polychrome bowl, discovered at Hilltop House, was used by Florence Hawley Ellis to illustrate three articles she wrote about in her master's thesis.

the University of Arizona. Chaco Canyon, New Mexico, became the focus of her excavation work. During the next two seasons she made a detailed study of fireplace charcoal, potsherds or pieces of pottery, and other materials uncovered in what had once been a refuse pile at Chetro Ketl. She had become interested in dendrochronology, a new field that examined tree rings in wood samples to pinpoint exact dates of everything from housing to fire pits. In 1929, she took one of the first courses on this subject, created by A. E. Douglass. This specialty, she later said, set her apart and helped her career as a woman in a man's field.

When the Depression hit and unemployment soared, Florence lost her job at the University of Arizona. In 1933, she took what small savings she had, loaded up her old Ford, and drove east—her first trip to a big city. She had been accepted as a scholarship student to work on her Ph.D. at the University of Chicago. Before she left, she'd already finished the initial draft of her dissertation using tree ring analysis and statistics, another new concept, to analyze the layers of discoveries she'd made at Chaco Canyon's Chetro Ketl. Again, her approach was considered innovative. Her findings were published in 1934, the same year she finished her doctorate.

When Florence wrote to see if she might get back her teaching job at the University of Arizona, she was told that the financial situation was not good. She assumed this meant no job. In desperation she applied to the small new Anthropology Department at the

Florence Hawley Ellis in 1974 at Mesa Verde National Monument. She did extensive studies in support of Pueblo land claims after retiring from teaching in 1971.

Mexico lasted until Florence's retirement in 1971. She taught more than two dozen courses in every area of anthropology, archaeology, and ethnology. During World War II she carried an especially heavy load of courses. When male teachers returned from the service, she found she was being paid "significantly less" than her male counterparts with less seniority. Promotion was slow and often discouraging.

In 1936, Florence married Donovan Senter. They had one daughter, Andrea, born in 1939. While her daughter was still very young, Florence conducted field research in the summer with teams of students. Her goal, she said, was to show students anthropology "wasn't just out of books." On occasion she brought her young daughter with her to interviews about kinship and social organization with native women. She found having a child with her helped make the women she spoke with feel more at ease. One Pueblo woman became Andrea's beloved godmother. Being a woman researcher, Florence later said, was not a handicap among the Pueblo people. She shared work, food, and confidences with them and came to be regarded as their trusted friend.

"My relationship to the Pueblo people has been influenced by the fact that I'm a woman," she said. "If you remain a woman in their eyes, they'll accept you. Women have a definite place and [they have] expected behavior in Pueblo society. Their place is more equal [to men] than in our society."

From 1937 to 1941, Florence carried a

University of New Mexico and was given a teaching contract. By the time she arrived in Albuquerque in 1934, she was so broke that she was forced to pawn her wristwatch and take a lien on her old Ford in order to pay her rent. She went out and bought a large yellow dog from a pound. It immediately ate her landlady's laundry, which was hanging in the backyard. Another expense she couldn't pay.

In spite of this inauspicious start, her teaching career at the University of New heavy teaching load in New Mexico while also teaching part of the school year at the University of Chicago, where she commuted to lead dendrochronology classes. She continued writing as well. Her book *Field Manual of Southwestern Pottery Types* (1936) became a classic reference for nearly half a century. For several years she and her husband cooperated on ethnological research. However, separation created by his enlistment in World War II and what she described as "perceived competition," even though they weren't in the same fields, caused marital problems. They divorced in 1947.

Two years later she met Bruce Ellis, an Air Force veteran who returned to the Southwest to take classes. They shared an interest in anthropology. In 1950, they married and she took his last name. He became a historian at the Museum of New Mexico in Santa Fe and later an editor of *El Palacio Magazine*, which has covered Southwestern art, history, and culture since 1913.

Florence led field expeditions in the summer across the Southwest at locations as varied as Chaco Canyon, old Pojaque Pueblo, Tsama Pueblo, and Mesa Verde. She directed a field school among the Alamo Navajo. In the mid-1950s, she began helping various indigenous peoples establish claims to land and water rights. She testified on land issues before the Indian Claims Commission on behalf of the Zia, Santa Ana, Jemez, Nambe, Taos, Acoma, Laguna, Hopi, and Santo Domingo.

Again, being a woman was not a problem. As she explained, "I think the Pueblo men think of women as being good advisors."

Florence felt very strongly about her commitment to her field. "Dedication to anthropology," she wrote, "is like dedication to one's religion; it is a way of life."

"Her working knowledge of the Southwest and its ties to Mesoamerica is phenomenal," wrote Theodore R. Frisbie, one of her former students who became a professor. "In total scope, there are few, if any, who can match it. Perhaps even more amazing is the fact that this woman is not only an academician, but also a warm human being who cares and is cared for in return."

After she retired, Florence became curator of what would one day be called the Florence B. Hawley Museum of Anthropology at Ghost Ranch Education and Retreat Center near Abiquiu, New Mexico—a striking landscape made famous by American painter Georgia O'Keefe, who lived nearby. The Hawley Museum displays 10,000-year-old artifacts from Paleo Indian cultures through ancestral Puebloan times to present-time pottery and weavings from local Pueblos. The museum houses the largest collection of Gallina artifacts in the world.

Florence never finished her 1,405-page opus on all the tribes of the Southwest, one of the many writing projects she pursued during her so-called retirement. "When I take time out to do some gardening," she wrote in a letter to a friend, "my conscience hurts because I am not writing, and then I write and begin to worry about the weather turning hot before the gardening is done."

Throughout her long career, Florence insisted on respect for data and scorned "easily dreamed up theories which do violence to it." She was a pathbreaker for many women in her field. She held strong opinions about what was necessary to succeed: hard work, dedication. "The producers are the workhorses, not the flash-in-the pan type," she wrote. "The best that is in us is sweated out onto paper and lives beyond our lifetimes. It is our sincere contribution to the world."

Florence Hawley died at age 84 on April 6, 1991. Hundreds of friends, relatives, and students—whites and Native Americans alike—attended her service. So many from the tribal council of Santo Domingo came to pay their respects that a bus had to be chartered. The ceremony was conducted in English and the native language, Keresan, and officiated by her adopted Zia son. "It was a tremendously moving tribute," wrote an attendee, "for one who had done so much for so many throughout her long and fruitful life."

CHAPTER SIX

Eleanor Margaret Burbidge

After decades of scanning the sky to observe the stars, astronomer Eleanor Margaret Burbidge was thrilled to finally glimpse a mysterious deep-space object she never thought she'd see in her lifetime. On October 28, 1990, she viewed on a computer screen at NASA's Goddard Space Flight Center the first image of a targeted quasar billions of light years from Earth. Quasar UM675, as it was called, appeared to behave like a star while sending out powerful, eruptive radio waves. What was this strange quasi-stellar radio source six million times fainter in appearance than a bright star that seemed to be speeding 150,000 miles per second away from Earth?

Nobody knew for certain. Margaret, as she was called, said that quasars were "real brain teasers" and referred to them as possibly "a new class of objects." "We've been waiting a long time," said Margaret, a self-described quasar hunter since they were first discovered in the 1960s.

What gave Margaret special satisfaction was that this quasar image had been successfully captured with equipment created under her leadership. The faint object spectrograph (FOS) was developed by her team of scientists at the Center for Astrophysics and Space Sciences at the University of California, San Diego. The FOS observes very faint objects in both visible and near ultraviolet regions of the spectrum. This was part of a complement of dedicated scientific instruments incorporated in the Hubble Space Telescope, which had been launched seven months earlier. Orbiting 375 miles above the Earth's atmosphere, the Hubble is the ultimate "clear skies" telescope—the kind that Margaret had yearned for throughout her long and remarkable career.

Her path to becoming one of the

Margaret Burbidge in 1980 viewing slides of galaxies and stars at an American Astronomical Society meeting. She was elected president of the American Association for the Advancement of Science that same year.

foremost astronomers in the world was not easy. During the early decades of her 70-year career, the field of astrophysics was dominated by men who controlled access to the most modern and powerful telescopes. As late as the mid-1960s institutions such as Mount Wilson Observatory in the mountains above Pasadena, California, and Palomar Observatory operated by California Institute of Technology in north San Diego County, California, refused women access to telescopes. The reason? The living quarters were purposefully designed to be a place "where male astronomers would not be bothered by their wives or families." Women astronomers also experienced systematic exclusion until the mid-1960s by the Carnegie Fellowships, the only funding available for study at Mount Wilson and Palomar. Like so many women astronomers, Margaret struggled to obtain research funding, professional recognition, promotions, and secure teaching positions.

Flexibility, stamina, and resilience were key to Margaret's success. "If frustrated in one's endeavor by a stone wall or any kind of blockage," she said, "one must find a way around—another route toward one's goal." This was advice she shared with countless young women scientists she mentored and inspired.

Born August 12, 1919, in Davenport, England, Margaret was the elder in a family of two girls. She grew up in a comfortable home in London near a huge park called Hampstead Heath. She and her sister enjoyed the attention of two maids and a nanny. They had dancing lessons, summer vacations in France, and plenty of books—ranging from *The World Book of Science* to *Treasure Island*, which she recalled made her "deliciously terrified."

Both of Margaret's parents were scientifically talented. Her father, Stanley, a chemistry professor nicknamed Old Peach Blossom by his students, became a successful research chemist and wealthy patent inventor. The family's wealth came from his process for creating vulcanized or hardened rubber.

Margaret's mother, Marjorie, had been one of Old Peach Blossom's students at the Manchester School of Technology. Seventeen years his junior, she was one of only a few women undergraduates. Marjorie's determination and her fascination with the flowers, plants, and trees of the natural world had profound impacts on Margaret. It was her mother who held four-year-old Margaret up to the porthole during a night crossing of the English Channel to distract her from seasickness by showing her the clear night sky. Margaret had never seen so many glittering stars. Her awe and wonder that August 1923 evening stayed with her all her life.

Her mother inspired Margaret in other ways as well. She encouraged Margaret and her sister to earn their own living "and not just be housewives," Margaret later recalled. This was unheard-of advice at a time when upper-middle-class women were told to marry well and not bother with college or a career.

Margaret's father gave her a pair of binoculars to view the night sky, a microscope, and (of course) a chemistry set. She became a passionate tree-climber. Fearlessness in scaling heights would serve her well later when she had to scale platforms to position telescope sights. Although she was bright and learned to read early, she was shy and hated school. What she loved were numbers—the bigger the better. She'd write a number with 120 zeros on a piece of paper and stare at it with what she called "enormous fascination." Passionate curiosity about mathematics would later drive her desire to know about the distances between stars, the vastness of deep space, and the origins of the universe.

Margaret attended an all-girls private prep school in London, where science equipment was limited but much emphasis was given to mathematics. While the school was strict, there was, she said, "no ban on nonconformity." Girls were never told they could not be scientists. An especially influential teacher inspired Margaret to work independently on physics experiments using a college textbook.

By the time she was 17, Margaret had already passed the necessary exams for college. That year marked the death of her father, who had long been an invalid. Enough money had been set aside for Margaret to attend whatever college she wanted. In 1936, she entered the University College of London, where she majored in astronomy and minored in mathematics. On the college grounds stood two

This stunning 2001 image from the Hubble Space Telescope revealed the heart of the Whirlpool Galaxy, the birth site of massive and luminous stars.

and provide mathematical calculations that analyzed Allied bombing surveys.

German nighttime bombing of British cities, called the Blitz, created nightmarish dangers for civilians from September 1940 to May 1941. More than a million homes were destroyed, and 40,000 civilians were killed, half of them in London. During the Blitz air-raid alerts, people hid in the subway and in special bomb shelters. To confuse Nazi pilots, blackout rules were strictly enforced in London and elsewhere. Windows were covered and outside lights were extinguished.

An unintended benefit of the blackouts was vastly improved telescope viewing. On nights when there was no bombing, Margaret stood or perched on a ladder in the enormous dome that covered the Wilson telescope and carefully studied the night sky. "While sitting on the observing ladder, I used to picture the star, its surface seething with turbulent outflowing gas." She imagined the stellar gravity, the rotation. "I used to picture those photons traveling through space and time, waiting for me or someone cleverer than me to make sense of the physics of the processes in the outer layer."

This thrilling experience fulfilled her early dreams and set up a pattern for the rest of her career. "I have never tired of the joy of looking through the slit in the darkened

small telescopes that provided her with her first real glimpse of distant stars on the rare nights that London skies were not cloudy or smoggy. Her experience with these telescopes inspired her to try to determine "the distance of as many stars as possible."

Margaret graduated from college in 1939, just as war erupted between Great Britain and Nazi Germany. "The world," she later said, "seemed to be turning upside down." With so many men enlisting in the army, jobs related to astronomy opened up for women for the first time. In 1940, she was hired northwest of London to maintain a 24-inch telescope dome and watching the stars," she later wrote.

As her research deepened, Margaret became fascinated by the origin of stars. Little was known about what they were made of and how chemicals reacted inside them. Like so many women scientists after World War II ended, Margaret lost her job in 1945 to a returning veteran. Unemployed, she decided to finish her Ph.D. Her goal was to find a place to work where she would have access to larger telescopes, better instruments, and the benefit of clearer skies. She wanted to go somewhere far from London, which had been badly damaged by bombs and was devastated economically.

Why not the United States? Eagerly, she applied for a Carnegie Fellowship that was supposed to fund young astronomers' use of telescopes at Mount Wilson Observatory. To her shock and dismay, she was told only men could use this high-tech telescope. Women were barred from Carnegie Fellowships, the rejection letter said. This was the first time she'd experienced discrimination because she was a woman.

Now what? She had to find another way.

During a graduate course in physics in 1947, tall, soft-spoken, ladylike Margaret met outspoken Geoffrey Burbidge, whom she called Geoff. He was described as "a large man with an even larger voice." His background was very different from hers. He was an only child born in 1925 in the Cotswold Hills between Oxford and Stratford-on-Avon.

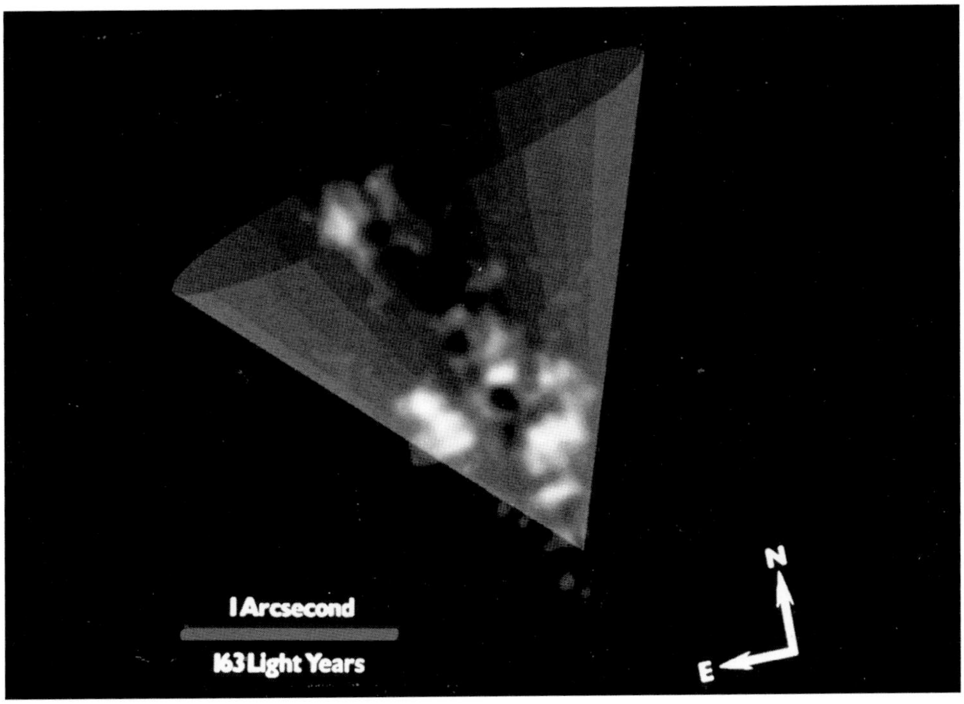

1 Arcsecond

163 Light Years

N

E

In 1990, the Hubble Space Telescope and Margaret Burbidge's Faint Object Spectrographic Investigation Team recorded this unprecedented, detailed view of highly energetic events in the core of a galaxy 30 million light-years away.

His father was a builder and his mother was a milliner.

Geoff was the first in his family to go beyond grammar school. He eventually received his Ph.D. in theoretical physics in 1951. His connection with Margaret changed his career ideas completely. After their marriage in 1948, he joined her on observing trips as her assistant. The physics of stars had always fascinated him. Later, he joked that he became an astronomer by marrying one.

Margaret changed her last name when she married Geoff, becoming E. Margaret Burbidge. She and her husband formed a research team dubbed B2 or B squared by their associates. Their work together—he did the theorizing, she did the observations—lasted more than 60 years, until his death in 2010 at age 84.

During their early years they led a nomadic existence, often surviving on minimal money, traveling as cheaply as possible, and living in college dormitories and wherever they could find affordable housing. They faced challenges securing access to the best telescopes and equipment, suitable academic and research jobs, and positions in the same city—sometimes even the same country. They traveled back and forth across the Atlantic, from England to the United States, and crisscrossed the American continent—a situation that caused them to delay starting a family.

Margaret made her first trip to the United States in 1950 with a grant to do research at the University of Chicago's Yerkes

Observatory in Williams Bay, Wisconsin, where women were not restricted from using the 40-inch refractor telescope. While Geoff worked at Harvard Research Observatory, she took the train from New York to Chicago and then on to Wisconsin. She said, "It was like entering a new world—literally a time of expanding horizons in all directions, physically, mentally, and spiritually."

Margaret focused her research on a specific group of stars called B stars. Soon her interests expanded to include understanding the structure of galaxies, what she called "the building blocks of the universe." She also spent time in the University of Chicago's sister observatory, McDonald Observatory, in Fort Davis, Texas.

In 1953, Margaret and her husband decided to investigate how chemical elements inside stars are created. Fred Hoyle of Cambridge University, a famous astronomer who was their friend, proposed that elements are constantly being created inside stars in a series of thermonuclear reactions. Nuclear physicist William Fowler from the California Institute of Technology joined the team. They worked together for the next four years to show how powerful, often violent reactions inside stars may have created elements that make up the universe: simple elements like pure hydrogen, helium, and lithium and elements like oxygen, iron, and the carbon-based building blocks of life as we know it.

The best place to collect data was Mount Wilson Observatory in California, where women were still forbidden to use the tele-

After being refused access to high-powered telescopes at Mount Wilson in California, Margaret Burbidge was able in 1951 to utilize the telescope at Yerkes Observatory, Williams Bay, WI, operated by the University of Chicago.

scope. Undaunted, Margaret was determined to gain access. In order to do the necessary observations and collect data, she posed as her husband's assistant. She had to work around all kinds of barriers that limited her observation time with the powerful telescopes and the sophisticated spectrograph, which recorded images of targeted stars. These images provided key clues about the stars' age and chemical makeup based on perceived color.

Margaret spent long winter nights in 1955 in the unheated observatory. She maneuvered the heavy ladder to reposition the telescope so that she could follow the targeted star as it appeared to move through the night. Mount Wilson rules made her work even more difficult. She and Geoff were not allowed to use the institution's only truck for transport up and down the mountain. She was forbidden to use the bathroom. ("Sorry, men only.") She and her husband could not eat in the dining hall and were told they had to live halfway down the mountain in a small, unheated summer cottage with no hot water.

Pregnant with their first child and worried that this would only be one more reason to forbid her access to badly needed observation data, Margaret tried to conceal her condition by wearing large, loose, warm clothing. By April 1956, however, she had trouble scrambling up and down and heaving the ladder around the platform. Her daughter, Sarah, was born in late 1956.

37-year-old Margaret continued to work on the data while her daughter was a newborn. A graduate student helped babysit. Margaret assisted in writing and editing her team's final 40-page report, "Synthesis of the Elements in Stars." Their theory came to be known as the B2FH theory from the first letters of its creators' names (Burbidge squared, Fowler, and Hoyle). Their findings rocked the scientific community when the article was published in 1957. The teamwork and research were among her most memorable accomplishments, she later said.

Their work showed in detail how different elements were produced by stars at different stages, providing a new view of the

Margaret Burbidge displays a photograph of a model of a telescope.

stead, she was offered an under-paid research fellowship. When the University of California set up a San Diego campus, she and Geoff jumped at the chance to go to this campus in 1962. Margaret was finally given a full professorship in 1964. She was 45 years old.

In 1971, her life changed again when she was offered the job of director of the Royal Greenwich Observatory, Great Britain's most famous observatory. She and her husband and 16-year-old Sarah left California in mid-1972 on a "leave of absence" in case they wanted to return. Margaret had suspicions and misgivings about the new job. No woman had ever been given the title of director of the Royal Greenwich Observatory, which is housed in a castle complete with a lush garden, a moat, and a pond full of swans. In past years this job had gone hand in hand with the title Chief Astronomer of England. This key role was, however, given to a man.

To make matters worse, the observatory was in the throes of a battle between young astronomers and the old guard. A dispute raged about what to do about moving a telescope out of England, where observations were possible only 600 to 800 hours per year because of foul, foggy weather. (By contrast,

galaxy as "a dynamic evolving organism, of stars that were an interacting community." Margaret and Geoff won the American Astronomical Society's Helen Warner Prize in 1959. Fowler was awarded a Nobel Prize in 1983 for his work on stellar nucleosynthesis.

In spite of their stunning success, Margaret still had trouble finding steady academic work with equitable pay. When the University of Chicago offered Geoff a job as associate professor, Margaret was told she could not be hired because of nepotism rules. In-the best viewing sites in the world ensure the telescope could be used 2,000 hours per year.)

After 15 months of strife, Margaret decided to resign and return to the United States to do what she loved most: research and observation with telescopes. She went back to California, where she filed for United States citizenship in 1977. She and Geoff returned to their jobs at the University of California, San Diego. She became very involved in promoting women's careers in science. She was elected the first woman president of the American Astronomical Society, 1976–1978, and the American Association for the Advancement of Science, 1983. In 1982 she was the Bruce Medalist, and in 1983 she won the National Science Foundation National Medal of Science.

Geoff, who had served as director of Kitt Peak National Observatory in Arizona from 1978 to 1984, died in 2010 at age 84 after a long illness.

Throughout her remarkable career, Margaret Burbidge remained a pioneer in her field. For many, she has been the quintessential role model for women in science. As Annella Sargent, a professor at Cal Tech, said, "She showed me early in my career that a woman could be an eminent scientist, have a successful family life, and accomplish all these things with grace and style."

ACKNOWLEDGMENTS

Many individuals helped me create SUPER WOMEN. Mike Buscher, Head, Reference Services, Geography and Map Division, Library of Congress; Debbie Bartolotta, Marie Tharp Estate; Marian V. Mellin, Lamont-Doherty Earth Observatory, Columbia University; Janelle Weakly, Arizona State Museum, the University of Arizona; Joyce Hawley; Emily Ray Brock, Palace of the Governor, New Mexico History Museum; Linda Seebantz, Ghost Ranch; David Atlee, Maxwell Museum of Anthropology, University of New Mexico; Flint L. Wild, NASA Education; Pablo Nelson, Astronomical Society of the Pacific; Kaitlyn Fusco, Mote Marine Laboratory and Aquarium; Ashley Morton, National Geographic Creative; Ann S. Turkos, University Archives, University of Maryland; Hannah Brown, Wellcome Library, London; Rebecca Williams, Duke University Medical Center Archives. Thanks also go to Mary Cash, super editor, for her encouragement and wisdom.

GLOSSARY

Anthropologist: person who studies the origins, physical and cultural development, biological characteristics, and social customs and beliefs of humankind

Antiviral drugs: class of medication used specifically for treating viral infections

Archaeology: the study of human history and prehistory through the excavation of sites and the analysis of artifacts and other physical remains

Astronomy: the scientific study of the universe around us, everything outside of the Earth's atmosphere

Astrophysics: the part of astronomy dealing with the physics and chemistry of astronomical objects and events

Atmosphere: the mixture of gases that surround a planet, moon, or star, held near it by gravity

Bacteria: one-celled microorganisms that multiply by dividing and can be seen only through a microscope

Biochemistry: a branch of science that explores the chemical processes within and related to living organisms. It is a laboratory-based science that brings together biology and chemistry.

Chemistry: a branch of physical science that studies the composition, structure, properties, and change of matter. This science deals with the composition and properties of substances and with reactions by which substances are produced from or converted into other substances.

Dendrochronology: a scientific method of dating events and variations in environment in former periods by comparative study of growth rings in trees and ancient wood

Ethnography: the study of human races and cultures

Ethnologist: an individual who studies what makes various human societies alike and different

Fathometer: a type of echo sounder used for measuring the depth of water. Echo sounding is a type of sonar used to determine the depth of water by transmitting sound pulses into water.

Galaxy: one of billions of large systems of stars and gas, held together by gravity, that make up the universe

Ichthyology: a branch of zoology or the study of animals that focuses on fishes, their structure, classification, and life histories

Immunology: a science that deals with the ways the body protects itself from diseases and infections

Marine biology: the scientific study of plants and animal life within saltwater ecosystems

Metabolism: the chemical processes by which a plant or animal uses food and water to grow and heal and make energy

Neurology: a branch of medicine dealing with the study and care of the nervous system, which includes the brain, the spine, and nerves throughout the body

Nucleic acid: a group of complex compounds that are vital to all living cells and viruses; molecules that carry genetic information directing how cells function

Oncology: a branch of medicine that deals with the prevention, diagnosis, and treatment of cancer

Penicillin: a medicine that destroys cell walls of bacteria to fight diseases

Petroglyphs: a drawing or carving on a rock or wall made by prehistoric people

Pharmacology: a science that deals with the origin, nature, chemistry, effects, and uses of drugs

Photon: a particle that cannot be seen with the naked eye and that has energy and movement but does not have mass or electrical charge; a subatomic particle that carries electromagnetic force; a discrete particle of radiant energy

Physiology: a branch of biology that deals with the functions and activities of life or of living matter; a biological study of the functions of living organisms and their parts, including all physical and chemical properties

Physics: a science that studies matter, energy, and their interactions

Plate tectonics: the study of how Earth's surface is in a constant state of change. Tectonic plates are massive, irregularly shaped slabs of solid rock that vary in size and thickness and that developed early in the Earth's 4.6 billion-year history. These plates drift on the Earth's surface like slow-moving bumper cars. Earthquakes and volcanic activity are concentrated near the boundaries of tectonic plates.

Protozoa: a diverse group of single-celled organisms

Quasar: a massive and extremely remote celestial object, emitting exceptionally large amounts of energy, and typically having a star-like image in a telescope. Recently it has been suggested that quasars contain massive black holes and may represent a stage in the evolution of some galaxies.

Spectrograph: an instrument that separates light into a frequency spectrum and records the signal using a camera

Spectrometer: an instrument that separates measurements into different energies or frequencies, producing a spectrum

Spectrum (plural spectra): the distribution of energy wavelengths and frequencies

Statistics: a science that deals with the collection, classification analysis, and interpretation of numerical facts or data

Theoretical physics: a branch of physics that employs mathematical models and abstractions of physical objects and systems to rationalize, explain, and predict natural phenomena. This is in contrast to experimental physics, which uses experimental tools to probe these phenomena.

Thermonuclear reaction: the process of combining two light atomic nuclei into a single heavier nucleus by a collision of the two interacting particles at extremely high temperatures, with the consequent release of a relatively large amount of energy

Velocity: quickness or rapidity of motion

Virology: a science dealing with the study of viruses and the diseases caused by them

Zoology: a branch of biology that studies animals and animal life

SOURCES

Ambrose, Susan, et al. *Journeys of Women in Science and Engineering: No Universal Constants*. Philadelphia: Temple University Press, 1997.

Babcock, Barbara A., and Parezo, Nancy J. *Daughters of the Desert, Women Anthropologists and the Native American Southwest, 1880–1980*. Albuquerque: University of New Mexico Press, 1988.

Bartusiak, Marcia. "Margaret Burbidge: Stars, quasars, supernovae, galaxies—if it's out of this world, she has seen it." *Smithsonian*, November 2005.

Boulton, Katherine. "The Nobel Pair." *New York Times Magazine*, January 29, 1989.

Burbidge, E. Margaret. "Watcher of the Skies." *Annual Review of Astronomy and Astrophysics*, September 1994.

Clark, Eugenie. "Into the Lairs of 'Sleeping Sharks.'" *National Geographic*, April 1975.

Clark, Eugenie. *The Lady and the Sharks*. New York: Harper & Row, 1969.

Clark, Eugenie, *Lady with a Spear*. New York: Harper & Brothers, 1953.

Clark, Eugenie. "Sharks: Magnificent and Misunderstood." *National Geographic*, August 1981, 148–9.

Clark, Eugenie. "Whale Sharks: Gentle Monsters of the Deep." *National Geographic*, April 1975.

Devorkin, David, and Smith, Robert W. *Hubble: Imaging Space and Time*. Washington, DC: National Geographic Society, 2008.

Duncan, Joyce. *Ahead of Their Time: A Biographical Dictionary of Risk-Taking Women*. Westport, CT: Greenwood Press, 2002.

Ellis, Florence Hawley. "Across Some Decades." *Ethnohistory*, vol. 18, no. 4 (Autumn 1971), pp. 295–307.

Ellis, Florence Hawley. *San Gabriel del Yungue as Seen by an Archaeologist*. Santa Fe, NM: Sunstone Press, 1989.

Ellis, Florence Hawley. "We Can Learn About Children from Them." *Parents Magazine*, July 1941.

Felt, Hali. *Soundings: The Story of the Remarkable Woman Who Mapped the Ocean Floor*. New York: Henry Holt, 2012.

Fox, Margalit. "Marie Tharp, Oceanographic Cartographer, Dies at 86." *New York Times*, August 26, 2006.

Frisbie, Theodore R., ed. *Collected Papers in Honor of Florence Hawley Ellis*. Norman, OK: Archaeological Society of New Mexico, 1974.

Frisbie, Theodore R. "Florence Hawley Ellis Obituary." *KIVA*, 1991.

Green, Timothy. "A Great Woman Astronomer." *Smithsonian*, January 1974.

Hall, Stephen S. "The Contrary Map Maker." *New York Times*, December 31, 2006.

Hodges, Jim. "She Was a Computer When Computers Wore Skirts." NASA interview, August 26, 2008.

Hunt, Richard. "Gertrude Belle Elion (1918–99), Pioneer of Drug Discovery." *Nature*, April 1999.

Kass-Simon, G., ed. *Women of Science: Righting the Record*. Bloomington, Indiana: Indiana University Press, 1990.

McGrayne, Sharon Bertsch. *Nobel Prize Women in Science: Their Lives, Struggles, and Momentous Discoveries*. Washington, D.C.: Joseph Henry Press, 1998.

North, Gary W. "Marie Tharp: The lady who showed us the ocean floors." *Physics and Chemistry of the Earth*, 35, vol. 35, June 8, 2010.

Overbye, Dennis. "Geoffrey Burbidge, Who Traced Life to Stardust, Is Dead at 84." *New York Times*, February 6, 2010.

Panek, Richard, and Ledner, Catherine. "Two Against the Big Bang." *Discover*, November 2005.

Polk, Milbry, and Tiegreen, Mary. *Women of Discovery: A Celebration of Intrepid Women Who Explored the World*. New York: Clarkson Potter, 2001.

Rossiter, Margaret, *Women Scientists Before Affirmative Action, 1940–1972*. Baltimore, MD: Johns Hopkins University Press, 1995.

Rutger, Hayley. "Remembering Mote's 'Shark Lady': The Life and Legacy of Dr. Eugenie Clark." Mote Marine Laboratory and Aquarium website: mote.org/news/article/remembering-the-shark-lady-the-life-and-legacy-of-dr.-eugenie-clark.

State of West Virginia Works Progress Administration Guide Series. New York: Oxford University Press, 1941.

Stone, Andrea. "'Shark Lady' Eugenie Clark, Famed Marine Biologist, Has Died." *National Geographic*, February 25, 2015.

Urry, Meg. "Girls and the Future of Science." The Blog. *The Huffington Post*, September 8, 2011.

Warren, Wini. *Black Women Scientists in the United States*. Bloomington, IN: Indiana University Press, 1999.

Warren, Wini. Interview with Katherine Johnson, March 6, 1996.

Wasserman, Elga. *The Door in the Dream: Conversations with Eminent Women in Science*. Washington, D.C.: Joseph Henry Press, 2000.

Yount, Lisa. *A to Z of Women in Science and Math*. New York: Facts on File, 1999.

Yount, Lisa. *Contemporary Women Scientists*. New York: Facts on File, 1994.

Yount, Lisa. *Twentieth-Century Women Scientists* (Global Profiles). New York: Facts on File, 1995.

WEBSITES
Academy of Achievement. Interview with Gertrude Elion conducted on March 6, 1991, in San Francisco, CA: http://www.achievement.org/autodoc/page/eli0int-1.

American Institute of Physics. Interview with E. Margaret Burbidge. https://www.aip.org/history-programs/niels-bohr-library/oral-histories/25487.

Goodsell Observatory, Carleton College website: https://apps.carleton.edu/campus/observatory/research/cindystudents/1998mn/history/mtwilson.

Mote Marine Laboratory and Aquarium website: mote.org/news/article/remembering-the-shark-lady-the-life-and-legacy-of-dr.-eugenie-clark.

NASA. "Alan B. Shepard Jr." https://history.nasa.gov/40thmerc7/shepard.html.

NASA. "She Was a Computer When Computers Wore Skirts." Article about Katherine Johnson. https://www.nasa.gov/centers/langley/news/researchernews/rn_kjohnson.html.

"NASA Statements on Katherine Johnson's Medal of Freedom," www.nasa.gov/press-release/nasa-statements-on-katherine-johnson-s-medal-of-freedom.

Society of Women Geographers. Oral history of Marie Tharp. http://www.iswg.org/resources/oral-histories.

West Virginia Archives of Culture and History. "Antebellum Slavery." http://wvculture.org/history/slavery.html.

Women's Museum of California. Margaret Burbidge. Trailblazer 2003. http://womensmuseumca.org/hall-of-fame/margaret-burbidge.

ADDITIONAL SOURCES
Maxwell Museum of Anthropology MSC01, 1050, 1 University of New Mexico Albuquerque, New Mexico 87131-0001

SOURCE NOTES

INTRODUCTION
"Do not let . . . you."
Academy of Achievement, unpaged

"The future . . . of gender."
Urry, unpaged

CHAPTER 1
Page

2   "Magnificent, misunderstood"
Clark, SMAM, pp. 148–9

2   "I pretended . . . sea."
Clark, LWAS, p. 4

4   "If you do . . . in you."
Ibid., pp. 41–2

5   "She took . . . very young."
Rutger, unpaged

6   "You have a . . . swimming."
Clark, LWAS, pp. 47–8

6   "I was alarmed . . . afraid."
Polk, p. 142

6   "I never . . . world."
Rutger, unpaged

7   "She gave . . . to."
Ibid.

"Her buoyancy. . . Pessimistic."
Stephens, p. 67

CHAPTER 2
8   "Congratulations . . . funny."
Academy of Achievement, unpaged

8   "I never . . . weird."
Ibid.

8   "for their . . . treatment."
McGrayne, p. 300

8   "more rational . . . processes."
Ibid., p. 302

9   "Everybody said . . . lives?"
Ibid., p. 295

10   "Self-effacing, gentle"
Ibid., p. 285

11   "Suddenly, it . . . wavered."
Ambrose, pp. 135–6

11   "too distracting"
McGrayne, p. 287

11   "I almost . . . discouraged."
Ibid.

11   "It really . . . before."
Ambrose, p. 137

12   "No question . . . women."
Ibid., p. 138

12   "I don't . . . much"
McGrayne, p. 289

12   "too elegant"
Ibid.

12   "She looked . . . dirty."
Ibid.

13   "I loved . . . to do."
Ambrose, p. 137

13   "This is . . . virology?"
Ibid.

13   "an evolution"
Ambrose, p. 138

13   "He told . . . do it."
Ibid.

13   "Pretty soon . . . grew."
Academy of Achievement,
unpaged

14   "I had . . . the one."
Ibid.

14   "Those of . . . crazy."
Ibid.

14   "are the results . . . happen?"
Yount, p. 54

15   "At first . . . excited."
Academy of Achievement, unpaged

15   "It's a . . . happier."
Ambrose, p. 140

15   "I think . . . succeed."
Wasserman, p. 49

15   "If we . . . lead us?"
Ibid.

15   "Every . . . than that."
Ambrose, p. 140

CHAPTER 3
17–18   "I have . . . space era."
Warren, NASA Interview

19   "Anything that . . . did."
Hodges, p. 14

20   "My dad . . . better."
Hodges, NASA interview

21   "We only . . . year."
Ibid.

22   "I had . . . NASA"
Warren, p. 145

22   "Let . . . heard."
Ibid., p. 144

CHAPTER 4
23   "It was . . . unmoving"
Society of Woman Geographers
unpaged

23   "absolutely horrified."
Ibid.

24   "girl talk"
Fox

24   "the most . . . cartography."
Ibid.

25   "making mud . . . nuisance."
Felt, pp. 27-28

25   "Terrible"
Ibid., p. 38

25   "I couldn't . . . blood."
Ibid., p. 38

26   "Not too . . . Hot."
Felt, p. 50

27   "something I . . . liked."
Felt, p. 50

27   "a once . . . opportunity."
Felt, p. 38

28–29   *National . . . famous.*
Ibid., p. 217

30   "How . . . see it."
Ibid., pp. 279–80

CHAPTER 5
31   "The movement . . . rush."
Ellis, p. 7

33   "In a . . . landscape."
Babcock et al., p. 125

34   "A pair . . . artifacts."
Maxwell Museum display case

37   "wasn't . . . books."
Babcock et al., p. 125

38   "My relationship . . . society."
Babcock et. al., p. 125

39   "I think . . . advisors."
Ibid.

39   "Dedication . . . life."
Ellis, p. 306

39   "Her working . . . return."
Frisbie, p. 10

39   "When . . . done."
Ibid.

39   "easily . . . to it."
Ibid.

39   "The producers . . . world."
Ibid.

38   "It was . . . life."
Frisbie, KIVA, p. 96

CHAPTER 6
40   "real brain teasers"
Green, p. 38

40   "a new . . . objects."
Yount, 20th Cent., pp. 44-5

40   "We've . . . time,"
Ibid.

41   "where male . . . families."
Goodsell Observatory

41   "If frustrated . . . goal."
Burbidge, p. 8

41   "deliciously terrified"
DeVorkin, interview

42   "and not . . housewives."
Burbridge, p. 8.

42   "enormous fascination"
Ibid.

42   "no ban . . . conformity."
Ibid.

43   "the distance . . . possible."
Ibid.

43   "The world . . . down."
American Institute of Physics,
unpaged

43–4   "While sitting . . . gas."
Burbridge, p. 7

44   "I used . . layer."
Ibid.

44   "I never . . . stars,"
Ibid.

44   "a large . . . voice."
Ibid.

45   "It was . . . spiritually."
Yount, A-Z, p. 27

45   "the building . . . universe."
Overbye, p. A28

46   "A dynamic . . .community."
Yount, A-Z, p. 26.

46   "She showed . . . style."
Women's Museum of CA

PICTURE CREDITS

INDEX

Page numbers in *italics* refer to illustrations

anthropologists/anthropology, 33, 36–39, 50
antiviral drugs, 14–15, 50
archaeological sites, 31–33, *33*, *35*, *36*, *37*, 39
archaeologists/archaeology, 31, 33–34, 36–38, 50
astronomers/astronomy, 40–49, 50
   see also observatories, astronomical
astrophysics, 41–42, 50
Atlantic Ocean, 23, 25, 27

Berann, Heinrich, 28–29, *29*
biochemistry, 8, 12, 14–15, 50
Black, Sir James W., 8
Burbidge, Eleanor Margaret, v, 41–49, *42*, *47*
Burbidge, Geoffrey, 45–49

Cape Haze Laboratory, 4–5
cartography, 24, 30
   see also maps and mapmaking
chemists/chemistry, 11–15, 31, 35, 43, 50
Clark, Eugenie, *iv*, v, *vi*, 1–7, *3*, *4*, *5*, *6*, *7*
computers
   electronic, 16, 18
   human, 16, *17*, 18, 22
continental drift, 23–24, 28
Cummings, Byron, 36–37

dendrochronology, 33, 37, 50
discrimination, *see* prejudice
Douglass, A. E., 37

Earle, Sylvia, 6–7
Elion, Gertrude, v, 8–15, *9*, *10*, *12*
Ellis, Florence Hawley, v, 31–40, *32*, *33*, *36*, *38*
ethnologists/ethnology, 33, 38–39, 50
Ewing, Maurice, 27, 28

Fowler, William, 46–47
Freedom 7, *ii*, 16–17, *18*, *20*
geologists/geology, 23, 25–26

geophysics, 24, 26
Glenn, John, 18
Gulf of Mexico, *3*, 4, 6

Heezen, Bruce, 23–24, 27–30
Hitchings, George, 8, *10*, 13–14
Hoyle, Fred, 46–47
Hubble Space Telescope, 41, *44*, *45*
human "calculators," 26
human "computers," 16, *17*, 18, 22

ichthyologists/ichthyology, 2–3, 50
Indian Ocean, *26*, 28

Johnson, Katherine Coleman, v, 16–22, *17*, *21*, *22*

Lamont Geological Observatory, 23, 26–28
Library of Congress, 29–30

maps and mapmaking, 23–24, *24*, 26, *26*, 27–28, *28*, 29, *29*, 30
marine biologists/marine biology, 2, 4–6, 50
mathematicians/mathematics, 16, 18, 21–22, 26, 43–44
Mercury (Project Mercury), 16, *19*
Mote Marine Laboratory and Aquarium, 5

NACA (National Advisory Committee for Aeronautics), 22
NASA (National Aeronautics and Space Administration), 18, *21*, 22, 41
National Geographic magazine, 28–29
National Geographic Society, 29–30
Navajos, 33, 39
Nobel Prize, 8–10, *12*, 15, 48
nucleic acids, 8, 13, 51

observatories
   astronomical, 41, 45–47
   geological, 23, 26–28
oceanographers/oceanography, 3, 6, 23
Office of Naval Research, 3, 29

oncologists, 14
oncology, 51

Pacific Ocean, 3, 7
petroglyphs, 33, 51
physics, 21, 51
physiology, 8, 51
plate tectonics, 24, 51
   see also continental drift
prejudice
   against African Americans, v, 18–22
   against Japanese Americans, v, 2–3
   against women, v, 2–3, 11–13, 18, 22, 24–27, 33–34, 37–38, 41–47
Project Mercury, 16, *19*
Pueblos
   archaeological sites, 31–33, *33*, *35*, *36*, 37, 39
   women's social position, 38–39

quasars, 41, 51

Red Sea, 4, *4*, 6, 7

Scripps Institution of Oceanography, 3
shark repellent, 6
sharks, *vi*, 1–3, *3*, 4–6
Shepard, Alan B., Jr., *ii*, 16–17, *18*
sonar recordings, 23, *24*, 26, 27, 28
spectrographs, 41, *44*, 45, 51

telescopes, 41, 42–45, 47, *47*
   see also Hubble Space Telescope; observatories, astronomical
Tharp, Marie, v, 23–30, *24*, *26*, *27*, *30*

virologists/virology, 14–15, 51

Whirlpool Galaxy, *44*
women
   position in Pueblo society, 38–39
   prejudice against, v, 2–3, 11–13, 18, 22, 24–27, 33–34, 38, 41–47

zoology, 2, 4, 51